THE SHED

Change your life by cleaning out your shed!

JO ETTLES

THE SHED: Change your life by cleaning out your shed!
Jo Ettles

Published by JoJo Publishing
First published 2014
Second Edition 2014

'Yarra's Edge'
2203/80 Lorimer Street
Docklands VIC 3008
Australia

Email: jo-media@bigpond.net.au or visit www.jojopublishing.com

© Jo Ettles

All rights reserved. No part of this printed or video publication may be reproduced, stored in or introduced into a retrieval system, or transmitted, in any form, or by any means (electrical, mechanical, photocopying, recording or otherwise) without the prior written permission of the publisher and copyright owner.

JoJo Publishing

Editor: Julie Athanasiou
Designer / typesetter: Chameleon Print Design
Printed in Singapore by KHL Printing.

National Library of Australia Cataloguing-in-Publication entry

Author:	Ettles, Jo, author.
Title:	The shed : change your life by cleaning out your shed / Jo Ettles.
ISBN:	9780987587985 (paperback)
Subjects:	Self-actualization (Psychology)
	Change (Psychology).
	Conduct of life.
	Orderliness.
Dewey Number:	158.1

DEDICATION

The Shed is dedicated to my father-in-law, who passed away in 1994. Somehow, since his passing, he has managed to continue to influence my life and my family's lives dramatically. *The Shed* is also a tribute to my mother and father, who for as long as I can remember showed me what you can achieve with a little determination and an organised vision. Being organised physically and mentally allows space to see, hear and experience life to the fullest. If your world needs a little spring cleaning, this book is a gentle reminder of how simple it is to live a purposeful life filled with peace and harmony. Every passing minute is an opportunity for you to open a new door. Just make sure you don't have to step over too many obstacles to get to it!

CONTENTS

Introduction 1

PART ONE: 5

One	What Are You Filling Your Shed With?	7
Two	A Message from Mystic Meg.	13
Three	The Exquisite Art of Nagging	17
Four	Sheer Passion	21
Five	Candle in the Wind (without the Wind).	27
Six	They're Never Really Gone.	33
Seven	Procrastination: It's a Curse	41
Eight	And the Healing has Begun.	45
Nine	The Symbolic Shed and its Message.	51
Ten	Honey, Don't Walk that Dog	57
Eleven	The Rhythm of Life: Can You Feel it?	67
Twelve	Self-Esteem: Are You Running on Empty?	73
Thirteen	YOU Make the Miracles.	81
Fourteen	The Power of Kindness.	85
Fifteen	Don't Play the Blame Game.	89

PART TWO: *Your 10 Steps Forward* 93

Step One	Clean Up Your House.	96
Step Two	Clear Out Your Mind	98
Step Three	Clean Out Your Body	102
Step Four	Spring Clean Your Soul	106
Step Five	Focus on What You Have.	108
Step Six	Write it Down	111
Step Seven	Stay Focused.	113
Step Eight	Repel Negative Energy	114
Step Nine	Soften Your Focus.	117
Step Ten	Start Your Affirmations and Change Your Life.	118

INTRODUCTION

Your home is your safe haven, your body is what carries you through this life, and your thoughts determine how you feel and respond to the world. Clearing each one of these areas out and filling them with love, laughter and beauty will bring your life immense joy. Mess and disorganisation according to feng shui principles is thought to create blockages and stagnant energy, and it also reflects a cluttered mind. Devoting time and energy to organising your surroundings and your life enables greater productivity and the potential for anything.

I have always been an extremely organised person. This is certainly an inherited gene from my dear mum. When I was growing up, Mum would always say to me (and to this day continues to remind me) that cleaning out one cupboard or doing one specific organisational task in your home every single day is completely therapeutic. She insists that it makes you see things more clearly and feel more in control, and it will lift your spirits even when your soul is feeling depleted. Mum is the most organised person I know. Watching her fill her days with so many accomplishments has taught me to manage my time effectively, ensuring that I can get the most out of my life.

Like many women, I can do a hundred things at once with confidence. In order to do these one hundred things, I have to be completely organised. My home needs to be organised, my time needs to be organised, and my mind needs to be organised. I have to prioritise when it comes to distractions. Fortunately for me, I can clean my teeth and clean the bathroom mirror at the same time. I can wipe the kitchen bench whilst putting away the dishes, and I can even straighten my hair while I am having breakfast. I love multi-tasking, especially when it comes to general cleaning duties. I like to get the daily chores out of the way first thing. This way I am free to fill my days with more enjoyable, productive activities. I know the same mess will have re-formed and be waiting to greet me on rising the next day, so I perform these necessary rituals with extreme speed.

I tend to work in time blocks during the day so I can achieve many things. My day has a beginning and an end, and the 'in-between' has a plan. The plan is filled with multiple achievements from minor to major and then when the day ends, it's tidied up and reviewed for closure over a glass of wine or two. Now don't get me wrong; there is plenty of chaos, plenty of stress and plenty of mess, but I always finish a task before I move onto the next and I try and follow my daily plan as best I can. By having a plan in my head, my mind stays clear and focused and I can achieve a plethora of activities in 24 hours.

Not everyone chooses to live this way. I choose to work in time blocks because I like to get the most out of my life. There are only 24 hours in one day, and I need to fit in family time, organising everyone time, work time, friend time, food time, exercise time and meditation time. What's that old saying? "There is never enough time in a day!" Time is a precious commodity, and I like to use mine wisely.

When it comes to being organised, I have friends who just wing it and fly by the seat of their pants from one day to the next. Some do it effortlessly, and some do it with gusto. I often visit one gorgeous girlfriend of mine, who shall remain nameless. Her home is filled with mess, both good and bad. If you drop in to visit Miss Messy for a mid-morning coffee when the kids are at school, she will still be in her pyjamas. Endless dirty dishes are covering her sink. There is spilt milk on bench tops, the television is blaring, and the radio is on. There are kids' toys all over the house, last night's rubbish is still waiting to be removed, dozens of books are half-read on the lounge, and washing in piles covering the floor. Everything from room to room is so wildly out of control that she doesn't know where it all begins and where it all ends.

Whenever I drop in to see Miss Messy, it's like her life is on hold. Have you ever seen the movie *Groundhog Day*? Every new day brings the exact repeat of the day before. There is so much mess surrounding her that she can barely take a step forward. I have only ever heard her refer to her days as being extremely challenging. She constantly complains that her life is a mess, her relationship is a mess, her kids are not coping at school, and she can't get a break. She feels like she is stuck on a merry-go-round and just can't get off.

I can see how overwhelmed she is, but if you look at her world, she is surrounded by chaos. There is so much of it in her home, in her personal life, and in her mind that she cannot think or see clearly. Miss Messy's world is overwhelming, and in her mind, it's a daunting task to sort it all out.

Each and every one of us is different when it comes to how we choose to live our lives and invest our time, but there is something calming and peaceful about organisation, both physically and mentally.

If your life feels like it is spiralling out of control, today is the perfect day to take the first step toward reorganising your life. Clean out your shed, tidy up your cupboards, de-clutter your lounge room, spring clean your office, and clear out your mind. Free up some space so you can fill your world with more love, laughter, goals and dreams!

"Lost time is never found again."
— **Ben Franklin**

PART ONE

CHAPTER ONE

What Are You Filling Your Shed With?

I have been married to my husband for 22 years. Just like all relationships, we have had our ups and downs, and as we get older and wiser, I am pleased to say that the ups are more often outweighing the downs. I knew from the minute I met him that he was my soul mate. How did I know? I just felt it. When we met, just for one moment, everything seemed to stop. There was an instant connection that was unexplainable. I felt a deep, natural affinity with him, and he made me feel safe and completely secure.

We are from different worlds, and are totally opposite. He loves the music of the eighties, and I like soul music. He loves motor bikes, Utes, beer and action movies. I love good wine, fashion and the arts. When it comes to food, he will order the largest steak on the menu or a kilo of ribs and devour them like a caveman. All the while I watch on in horror as his arteries harden. He eats with enthusiasm and appreciates every mouthful. I on the other hand will pick and fuss, count the calories, and consider the reaction my body will have after I have eaten. I rarely eat red meat, and I am constantly working on finding the right blend of nutrition that suits my delicate digestive system. Somehow, despite our likes and dislikes, we are able to meet in the middle and respect each other's individual passions.

My husband is a Virgo, and I am a Pisces. A classic textbook

Pisces, I display typical Piscean traits like imagination, sensitivity, creativity, compassion and intuition.

Virgos on the other hand are typically modest and shy. Meticulous and reliable, intelligent and analytical, Virgos are renowned for their perfectionism. Often they are criticised for their attention to detail and compulsive, almost obsessive desire for excellence when it comes to organisation.

Here's where things get confusing. My husband is definitely reliable, and I can always count on him. He is my rock. He sorts everything out, eventually. He is intelligent for the majority of the day but then that part of his brain turns off at around 7pm when beer and TV allow the Virgo male's mind to reboot. He is analytical and will go to the ends of the earth to solve a problem. Is he shy? I don't think so. He has no problems working a crowd or bringing a dinner party together, and he will talk to everyone and anyone easily and make them feel special. The tidy trait—well, that has been seriously overlooked, and had you seen his shed before this book was created, you would have certainly questioned the theory behind the 12 signs of the zodiac.

My Virgo male has a habit of starting a project and never quite finishing it completely. Hence, our life reflects many projects, from business to building, that never see their full potential due to an enthusiastic start followed by an 'I am over it' ending. Looking back over the years, had we put all that energy into seeing just one long-term project from start to completion, I am sure we could have conquered the world!

If there is a problem or task to solve, I like to face it, acknowledge it, resolve it, complete it, and then move on. A problem unsolved consumes way too much precious energy. My Virgo male has a slightly different view. He thinks if you ignore a problem or cover up an unfinished project, it will magically disappear. His definition for complete is that if you don't complete a job but do almost all of it, this qualifies it as somehow completed.

This theory is reflected in our home. We live in a very old timber house. It's a traditional Queenslander-style home that is around 80 years old. We purchased it over 10 years ago, and we saw huge potential for a transformation into a more modern-style space still accented by the house's classic Queenslander features.

Ever the enthusiastic team that we are, we planned to do this renovation rescue ourselves. This would include raising the house to a legal height and enclosing the underneath to incorporate more rooms as well as ripping out the very ugly bathroom. Our enthusiastic vision did not really take into account the cost of the renovation. My Virgo male believed that somehow we would bring it all together and magically the finances would appear. So, Project 'Make This House a Home' commenced with enormous hope and an exciting vision for a great result on a very small budget.

Now, let me make the following point clear. No plans were drawn up or prepared to create this vision. All the plans were carefully stored in my Virgo male's brain. I continuously asked for information on what he was envisaging for the layout and was hoping that we were visualising a similar place, but my Virgo male had his plans carefully locked away in his cerebellum and was certainly cagey about releasing them to me.

Regardless, I was going to assist him as all good trades assistants do and trust that he knew what he was doing. Project 'Make This House a Home' commenced, and within eight weeks, under my Virgo male's guidance, we had raised this old Queenslander to new legal heights. It was now ready for the big transformation from a one-storey house to a two-storey home. After each weekend of working on this massive building project, my Virgo male would put down the tools, step back, and soak up his amazing talents as a home renovator over a cold beer. We would both relax on the grass, beer in his hand and glass of wine in my hand, and we would relish in the satisfaction of our achievements. What's that old saying? Oh, that's right, "There is great satisfaction in doing a job yourself". I am still unsure about the validity of that statement as deep down inside, I think there would have been greater satisfaction in paying a builder while we holidayed in Tahiti.

Each weekend, after my Virgo male reviewed his 'Tim the tool man' skills and grunted with satisfaction at his own awesomeness, he would high five himself with his beer-free hand and then proceed to put his tools in the shed for safe-keeping until the following weekend. He would be quite exhausted at this point and would carry the tools around to the infamous shed, open the doors, and hurl them inside with vigour. Each Sunday afternoon at around 5pm, this ritual would occur. All the while, additional supplies for our renovation were being purchased and stored in this very small shed during the week.

Years of memories, hobbies, and incomplete projects were stored in boxes at the back of the shed. Our favourite books, tennis rackets, diving gear, toys, blackboards, electric scooters, skateboards, bikes, golf clubs, fishing rods, crab pots, broken computers and electrical gear all piled high, teetering and touching the roof.

If you sneezed while standing inside the shed, there was a serious risk that the four tin walls would just collapse outwardly and our whole lives would be exposed to the elements. Now on top of all these contents, please add one

CHAPTER ONE

lawn mower, one edger, one whipper snipper and endless amounts of saw dust! I had attempted on a number of occasions to clean out and reorganise the infamous shed so I could at least pull out the mower without injuring myself, but before I attempted these clean-ups, I would always feel a little nervous about what frightening creatures may be lurking inside the shed. We have some of the deadliest animals in the world living in Australia, so before entering the shed, I would always consider which ones were most likely to be hiding in this 3-metre by 3-metre silver storage unit.

At the top of this list was the taipan, a large, fast and highly venomous snake found in Australia. The taipan has the most toxic venom out of all the snake species worldwide. This snake is usually found in Australia's Far North Queensland — and in case I didn't mention it, Far North Queensland is where we live. Apparently, the taipan loves hanging out in sheds. Next on my list of inhabitants was the redback spider, Australia's deadliest spider. Although commonly favouring toilet seats as its place of residence, it has been known to frequent sheds.

Let us not forget the brown snake either. The brown snake produces venom, which quickly kills if it goes untreated. Even young snakes are capable of delivering a fatal bite to humans.

There is also the tiger snake, another venomous snake found in Australia. My neighbour had found one under her bed once. The snake catcher said it had been sleeping under my neighbour's bed for at least a week and she was extremely lucky she had not been bitten. She proceeded to drink copious amounts of alcohol for a solid week after that experience, and as good supportive neighbours, we joined her in drinking plenty of wine to help her through this terrible shock. Obviously, I now check daily to ensure that there are no snakes residing under our bed.

Let's not exclude the funnel web spider either. The funnel web is a darkly coloured spider resembling a tarantula and has huge fangs full of venom. This is one ugly, dangerous creature and could certainly be a resident of the shed. When reviewing the possible risks associated with cleaning up a shed Down Under, consideration had to be given to the fact that not just one but all five deadly creatures could be settled comfortably inside.

The shed was a potential death trap! Despite the dangers, however, I did manage on a number of occasions to reorganise the shed so that you could walk in and find tools without breaking your neck. But lo and behold, it always seemed to return to its original state sooner rather than later. I am not talking about organised chaos but complete chaos. There were a number of closets, chests and rooms in our home that looked very similar to our shed. No matter how hard I tried to keep them organised, they would always end up totally overloaded with useless items and broken and unfinished project parts. Needless to say, these particular cupboards and areas belonged to my beloved Virgo male.

> *"Chaos in the world brings uneasiness,*
> *but it also allows for opportunity and growth."*
> —**Tom Barrett**

CHAPTER TWO

A Message from Mystic Meg

Some years ago, a girl I was working with came into my office bubbling with excitement after visiting a local clairvoyant. The clairvoyant had given her hope for the future in the areas of love and finances. My colleague said, "You have got to go see her. She is amazing." Her reading was clearly everything she had hoped for because she was ready and waiting for her soul mate to come bursting into our office. Apparently, he was coming very soon!

Curiosity got the better of me, and I was keen to hear some positive predictions relating to my own future. Things had been particularly challenging of late, so I was hopeful that a financial fortune and an overseas trip were just around the corner! I called the clairvoyant, scheduled an appointment, and got really excited about what might be in store for me. My reading day came. I headed over to the clairvoyant's house, keen to hear her predictions.

I knocked on the door of the old home and a tiny, elderly, European lady came out to greet me. She would have been at least 75 years of age. She was short and plump with greasy, dark hair, and she spoke in a thick European accent. "Come in, come in and sit down," she said in a matter of fact sort of way. She asked me to shuffle some cards and select the ones I was drawn to for her to read. She sat quietly whilst I sat in anticipation. After a few minutes, she blurted out, "You and your husband are soul mates". I thought that was nice and a great way to start my reading, but I was already aware of this. I wanted to hear the exciting stuff. She then proclaimed, "You are both boring". She was so blunt, and she stifled a yawn as she said it. I thought "Oh God!" Seriously, we are not that boring. Most people find us very engaging. She then yelled at the top of her lungs, "I like to read for people who are interesting".

"What the devil? This woman is crazy!" I thought. She went on to say that she liked to read for people who were having affairs and who were a little sordid as it was far more interesting. As I was doing none of that, she was finding the whole experience of reading for me very mundane. Well, that was a relief, I suppose!

Her next prediction was a little more disturbing. She shouted, "You will drop dead when you are 75! You will be in the kitchen doing the dishes, and then BANG! GONE!" I thought, "Oh my goodness! She is tactless". I started calculating how many years I had left to do the dishes, and it was just 33.

She said that my partner would pass some years after me, but I was first to go. I did feel slightly panicked, and I couldn't help thinking that a reputable clairvoyant would more than likely keep that little snippet of insight to themselves to ensure her client does not run out, screaming in fear. Just for the record—note to self and my Virgo male—I will not be doing the dishes in the year 2038. At this point, I had decided that I did not like this clairvoyant.

She went on to give me the normal predictions associated with readings. I would have grandchildren, a friend would divorce, a friend would go broke, and I would have two surgical procedures—clearly before I dropped dead at 75. Finally, she asked, "Is that it? Do you want to know anything else?"

I responded firmly with, "No, I really don't think so," and I stood up to leave. She then said, "By the way, tell your husband to clean out his shed. When he does this, luck will come back into your lives". She snatched the 50 dollars I was holding in my hand and ushered me to the door, where her next victim was waiting. I wanted to tell them to run for their lives, but she dragged them inside before I could warn them.

When I got home, I opened up the shed. Mystic Meg was accurate with that particular message for sure. The shed was a mess, but I honestly thought her parting message related to a feng shui principle. Clearly, our shed was sitting on a very important space blocking the positive energy from flooding into our lives. Cleaning and organising it would obviously improve our world, according to Mystic Meg. I decided it was time to get my Virgo male to clean up! I was desperate to experience good fortune before I dropped dead at 75. Little did I know that it would take six years to clean up that shed and six years before the clairvoyant's parting words became clear! By the way, my colleague is still waiting for her soul mate.

> *"The future belongs to those who believe in the beauty of their dreams."*
> —**Eleanor Roosevelt**

CHAPTER THREE
The Exquisite Art of Nagging

I could hardly wait for my Virgo male to get home from work that afternoon. After visiting the clairvoyant, I was busting to let him know how simple it was going to be to change our lives. I explained to him that all he had to do was tidy up his shed, and the luck would come flooding in. Things had been tough for a few years, so I was extremely keen to change this pattern.

We discussed my reading over a few drinks on our deck, and after drink number four, we had convinced ourselves that a simple clean-up would bring us a huge lottery win, a yacht, and a Mercedes C-Class Coupe. After drink number five, we had paid off all of our families' mortgages, made many anonymous donations to charities, and organised a family reunion in Perth with George Michael entertaining us all at the event. By drink number six, I was Googling Tony Bennett's email address as we were making plans to invite him to serenade mum and dad at the big family reunion with his rendition of "I Left My Heart in San Francisco".

My Virgo male was equally as excited as I was and planned to hit the shed on the weekend for a big clean-up. The potential of unblocking our obvious good luck blockage was almost overwhelming. It seemed simple enough, and we were both ready for some serious positive energy to flow back into our lives.

The Shed

The weekend came, and then it went. Not much was achieved, as my Virgo male couldn't quite get it together to face the shed head on. Any spark of motivation to tackle the job at hand was quickly annihilated every time the shed doors were opened. At one point I saw my Virgo male open the shed doors and then close them again. He then proceeded to the garden and began vigorously weeding. He was cutting branches off trees, sweating, puffing and grunting. He was looking really busy, but he was not actually making a noticeable difference to the environment.

"How's that shed clean-up going?" I asked.

"Getting there!" he yelled.

As I said, that weekend came and went, and still the old shed remained obviously dishevelled. I would gently remind my Virgo male of what was in store for us after the clean-up, and I would see the excitement in his face. My Virgo male would always respond with, "I will surely get into it tomorrow."

Tomorrow would come, and tomorrow would go. My gentle questioning and words of encouragement seemed to be getting louder and more frequent. My nice, sweet tone had changed somewhat, and now I was sounding more like a woman possessed by some evil creature. Had my head started to rotate like Linda Blair's had in the movie *The Exorcist*, it would have come as no surprise.

Week in, week out, and that shed remained in turmoil. I became more and more frustrated. I continued to remind my Virgo male that because he had not heeded Mystic Meg's warning to clean up the shed, it was his fault that we had not won the lottery. It was also his fault that George Michael and Tony Bennett had not friended me on Facebook. I begged and pleaded with my Virgo male to clean up the shed with little success.

Finally, I decided to take matters into my own hands. I donned my protective outdoor clothing and started to clean up the shed. From top to bottom, I stacked and tidied, disposed and cleared, and reorganised the mess. Everything inside had a spot. I thought, "Finally, I have cleared this space." According to the law of feng shui and Mystic Meg's message, the path was now well and truly open for positive energy to flow into our lives.

I threatened my Virgo male with divorce if he messed up that shed. It had taken me three solid days from sunrise to sunset to achieve organisation. I was so proud of how tidy it was that I could barely contain myself. I closed the doors and felt completely confident that soon our lives would change for the better all because that shed was clean! I was ready for the universe to unleash its flow of abundance right out of those shed doors and into our lives. Goodbye hard times, hello good times! Universe, bring it on!

> *"Doing what you love is the cornerstone of having abundance in your life."*
> —**Wayne Dyer**

CHAPTER FOUR

Sheer Passion

I had remained confident that my Virgo male would keep the shed tidy as divorce would have been a messy option for him and one I was sure he would want to avoid. I did not go down to the shed for weeks. I was busy with work, so a visit to the shed was not necessary. Things continued to be quite stressful in our lives, and we were challenged daily by what seemed to be an unusually prolonged run of bad luck.

The company I worked for went into receivership. Our son contracted Dengue fever. My Virgo male was riding his motorbike to work, hit a wallaby, and suffered some serious injuries that left him out of commission for six weeks (although sadly, the wallaby did not survive). The company my Virgo male worked for went into receivership just after I lost my job. Our son needed a simple routine operation, just a day surgery, which ended with major complications. The engine in our car blew up within a week of the operation, and the car never worked again! Our one very special holiday planned overseas was cancelled due to a volcanic eruption off an island south of Bali, our holiday destination. We got as far as Darwin on this trip, we were stuck in the airport for four days, and we returned home.

Three days after our return, our hometown was under threat of a major cyclone. One of the worst cyclones in history was expected to hit. Fortunately, the cyclone was downgraded from a category five cyclone to a category three cyclone. We did suffer some structural damage due to the intensity of the storm but not nearly what we had expected. The day after the cyclone, we were cleaning up the debris caused by the winds and our home was struck by lightning. Actually, that event was more terrifying than the cyclone and caused a lot of damage. In fact, a few minutes later, the house across from us was also hit by lightning, and its roof tore open.

During all of these challenges, my Virgo male finally secured some casual work. It lasted four weeks as the global recession crucified the construction industry in our town. A lot of major construction companies went bankrupt, leaving countless men unemployed. I could continue to keep listing the dramatic events that kept rolling in, but I think you get my drift. We were going through a very negative cycle in our lives, and it wasn't like these events happened over a decade—they happened over a few months! On the bright side, we were all fit, well, and together, so regardless of the challenges coming our way, we were extremely grateful for this enormous blessing.

We all have negative cycles in our lives, and if you are experiencing one at the moment or have been through some tough times of late, I am sure that you can relate to the feeling that the whole world is against you. During our 'annus horribilis', I can assure you that we definitely felt that the whole world was against us. It was one blow after another without a break in-between to catch our breaths or refocus.

You can try to analyse it, rationalise it, and justify it, but it is often too overwhelming to comprehend. My Virgo male and I have always had the ability to get straight back up when knocked down. You know that song, "When the Going Gets

Tough" by Billy Ocean? Well, that is our mantra. We have always believed that when the going gets tough, the tough get going. Challenges make you stronger, and you learn something from every single one. We have always encouraged each other and pulled each other out of any pity parties. There were countless days during our rough patch, however, where neither of us had anything left to give. Every challenge seemed insurmountable, and because of the unrelenting occurrences, we felt exhausted. Consequently, we were overwhelmed, and as a result, many other aspects of our lives became messy because we were so focused on these huge dilemmas that were occurring.

Regardless of those trying days, we still managed to refocus and acknowledge that there was always someone far worse off than ourselves. You only have to read a newspaper or watch a news report to realise that if you are healthy and loved, have access to clean water and food, and live with freedom, you are truly blessed.

On a whim, I decided that perhaps a splash of colour in our kitchen would change the energy around us and bring in some luck. You know, a change is as good as a holiday, and we certainly needed both. I went to the paint shop and stood pondering over colour samples. I had a feeling that one of the paint tins contained the power to spark a rainbow with a pot of gold at the end of it.

Finally, after an hour of procrastinating, I decided that it was time to be bold. I chose a beautiful hue called 'sheer passion' for our kitchen. This lovely paint can only be described as a rich, warm, mulberry-red tone. It definitely had the potential to bring a fresh new feel into our home, one that would hopefully bring with it a more positive energy. In China, red symbolises prosperity and joy, so based on that information, 'sheer passion' was definitely the colour for us.

I went up to the hardware assistant, and I said to him, "I would like some sheer passion for my kitchen, please." He replied cheekily, "And I would like some sheer passion in my kitchen, please!" He mixed up my paint with such gusto and enthusiasm, it was as if he was preparing colour for a renaissance masterpiece. He carefully added, blended, shook, and then added more colour to my tin, and all the while he was smiling and saying, "Ah, beautiful, beautiful."

After he had lovingly prepared my blend, he took off the lid and showed me the result. He seemed so proud of his creation of colour. "Now that should bring some passion, richness and inspiration into your home," he declared. I was feeling inspired already!

The hardware assistant's positive approach to mixing my paint had only added to my excitement. It was as if he had followed the paint recipe as instructed by the paint manufacturer and then added his own special blend of creative artistic talent and emotion to mix up more than just a tin of paint. His enthusiasm and love of colour flowed into my tin of sheer passion, and I just knew that I was about to bring something special into my home!

I raced home with my tin of paint. My Virgo male was not so sure about the colour and was clearly nervous about change, but I was only painting one feature wall, so how much damage could I do? The next day, my Virgo male was leaving to go away to a mine site in Mount Isa for a fortnight of work. At that stage, with such high unemployment in our town, we grabbed opportunities like this with both hands. Separation was easier than bankruptcy. I decided to do the painting while he was away. That way, he would come back to a home that had a new motivating, inspirational feel to it. There was a lot riding on my tin of sheer passion!

CHAPTER FOUR

The next day, I was up early preparing myself for a day of painting. The paint was open and stirred, my paint clothes were on, the drop sheets down, and now I just needed to get my brushes, paint roller and paint tray from the shed. I headed downstairs and stood at the shed doors. The shed looked extra shiny, bright and inviting for some reason. I knew that my painting equipment was located approximately one meter in and on the right hand side of our shed. I knew this because I had spent three days making sure that we could locate any item we needed with ease and speed. Also, I was confident that when I stepped inside the shed, I would feel the positive energy flowing up from the ground and pulsating through every spanner, hammer and whipper snipper carefully arranged in and on this sacred ground.

I unlocked the padlock, pulled out the handle and swung open the shed doors. Now if this book had sound effects, right about now, you would hear the theme song from the movie *War of the Worlds*, the first few dramatic bars of which so intensely elicits an image of shock, devastation and the aftermath of what would happen if aliens really did invade the world. In this case, it appeared that aliens had possibly invaded the shed.

I was faced with what seemed to be a scene of mass destruction. The organised shed now resembled an area that the government would declare a disaster zone. Had there been an explosion inside? Had a wild beast got into the shed and gone crazy trying to escape? I could not for the life of me understand how this recently-organised storage area had been transformed into an area of such turmoil.

As I gradually stepped further inside, it was clear. There had been no aliens. There had been no wild beast. This looked like the work of one Virgo male! Suddenly, any hope of my

25

Virgo male experiencing 'sheer passion' from his wife on his return from the Outback was squashed!

> *"Colors, like features,*
> *follow the changes of the emotions."*
> — **Pablo Picasso**

CHAPTER FIVE
Candle in the Wind (without the Wind)

It was now very obvious, in my opinion that this particular area of storage was once again somehow contributing to the chaos in our lives. It seems silly, doesn't it? Any rational human being would think that the above statement is just nonsense. How could a messy shed be contributing to our chaotic lives?

Drinks with the girls and discussions about our beloved spouses' sheds revealed that there were many storage areas around North Queensland in disarray. Stories were emerging about these male domains and how messy they were. There was a common thread amongst all these stories, however; although many of these sheds were in a mess, most husbands knew where everything was located inside their sacred storage area. What was alarming for me was that my Virgo male did not know where anything was located in our shed. He would buy a special tool, and once it was placed inside the shed, it was never seen again.

Time passed, our shed remained dishevelled, and our lives remained consistently challenged. I had decided to call a truce, wave the white flag in surrender, and accept the fact that my Virgo male's messy shed was not typical of the traits of your normal Virgo personality, and I would have to learn to live with it. My new motto was, "Out of sight, out of mind." I made a pledge to never enter the shed again! I would focus my attention on finding another way of bringing a change into our lives.

One day, I went to a store to buy some candles and scented oils to burn in our home. The store was a very tiny shop located in a big shopping mall. It was owned by a local clairvoyant. People would pay him to read for them. I definitely wasn't interested in doing that. Mystic Meg had given me enough information to keep me checking my cholesterol, blood pressure, and heart health for a while!

I just loved his range of candles and beautiful oils that he sold. They always brought a feeling of calm into our home. I have to admit that I am slightly addicted to burning candles and oils as they seem to turn any cold space into a warm space. I stood quietly, carefully inhaling his range and just waiting for that special scent to overwhelm my senses.

Mr Clairvoyant came over to me and asked if he could help me with anything. I informed him that I was fine and I was very happy browsing. He acknowledged my response but continued to stare at me with a really odd expression on his face. I thought to myself, "Am I wearing too much blush today?" I didn't have my contact lenses in, so anything was possible.

After a few minutes, he apologised for staring and then said to me, "Goodness, I have to tell you that you have this light around you and you have an amazing gift. If you use it wisely, you can help many people." At that point, I couldn't see the light around me, but I was very impressed with his intro sales pitch. Clearly, he was dangling a carrot in front of me in the hope of enticing me to ask for some more enlightening information. Not a bad opening line to get me to cough up 50 dollars for a reading.

I was definitely not going down that road again, so I thanked him and selected a beautiful candle to burn in our home. I paid for the candle, and he continued to stare at me. As I thanked him again and bid him a great day, he gave me one more parting statement that left me slightly breathless. He looked at me with intent and said, "Your husband needs to clean up that mess at the front area of your home. It's not what you think, but when it is done, only then will your lives change, allowing you to move forward. I stress again, it's not what you think." I was left speechless, which is unusual for me because I am rarely lost for words. Once again, this damn shed had re-emerged and was the focus of our continuing bad luck. I walked away from the store with my candle, and I was definitely tempted to turn around and ask the clairvoyant about my future, but I continued forward with a new enthusiasm. It was time to sort this mess out once and for all.

On my Virgo male's return from work that evening, we sat on our balcony with a glass of wine. We have a very picturesque backyard that is teaming with tropical butterflies, palm trees, and an enormous pool with a cascading waterfall—it is truly a serene space. I try never to take this natural beauty for granted and the feeling of contentment it has brought me since we have lived here. I have often dreamt that I have had to move out of this house, and I have woken up with tears streaming down my face. I really felt the sadness through my dream.

There was something different about this particular evening, though. I told my Virgo male about what had happened that day and the message Mr Clairvoyant had passed on to me. I went and got my recently purchased candle and placed it on the table that we were sitting at. I lit the candle for no reason other than to experience its scent on a beautiful night overlooking our little tropical oasis.

We sat chatting about life and its struggles. We both tried to understand why our shed was continuously popping up as a very negative area. We tried to make sense of the strange coincidental messages and their meanings. There had to be something in these two very similar statements, as weird as they were. It just didn't seem logical, though. How could our messy shed be stopping us from moving forward and experiencing a more positive life?

We were enjoying the evening, and as night fell and the moon started to rise, there was a moment. This moment felt almost surreal, and even my very practical Virgo male felt it. For just one moment, the candle seemed to burn brighter than before. The scent was sweeter and stronger, and the flame seemed to flicker and dance, yet there was no breeze. The moonlight seemed to shine right down onto our balcony, encasing just the table, the candle and us. It was so bright that it was impossible to ignore its glow.

We both looked at each other and—call it the moonlight, call it the wine, call it what you will—we both felt an energy surrounding us that was unexplainable. This energy bought no blame and no fear, just clarity. In that moment we felt completely surrounded by peace. The candle flickered enthusiastically, and without reason we began to talk about my husband's father, who had passed away in 1994. Ted was such a lovely man who was so proud of his two sons and his lovely daughter. His infectious smile could light up an entire room, and he was forever encouraging all of us to go for gold. You could always count on him for advice and reassurance, no matter what the situation. He made sure that we all knew he was always there for us.

He was continuously hugging his kids and telling them how much he loved them. It was as if perhaps he knew that he had to make it count while he had the chance. His health had deteriorated dramatically in his last year on earth, yet his smile never ever faded and his big heart continued to radiate warmth and love right up until he passed. Losing him left a huge hole in everyone's lives.

We sat at our table that evening, and for the very first time, my Virgo male really expressed his sadness and the sense of loss that came with his dad's passing. His father was the one person who had always been there for him. He taught him how to fish and how to cook. He showed him what it is to be honourable and how to live his life with integrity. He had always been there to guide my Virgo male through the tough times, encourage him through the lean times, and continuously challenge him to finish what he started no matter how hard the journey.

He was never afraid to pull my Virgo male into line! He would hound my Virgo male to go forward, clean up his mess and go the distance. He would always offer solid advice when sorting through life's challenges. My Virgo male would just pick up the phone whenever he needed his dad to encourage him through bad times. My Virgo male was 29 years of age when he lost his dad. It was a huge blow to him to lose the one person he instinctively trusted to guide him throughout his life.

As the candle continued to burn brightly at our table, we both acknowledged that my Virgo male had felt like he had somehow lost his teacher, his mentor and his support system when his dear dad had been taken from him all those years ago. He had never really talked about it or accepted it, and it was very clear that his dad's departure had left a huge void in his world. The one person he relied on to steer him through his life was gone.

"Perhaps they are not stars, but rather openings in heaven where the love from our lost ones pours through and shines down upon us to let us know they are happy."
—**Eskimo Proverb**

CHAPTER SIX

They're Never Really Gone

I personally believe that when a loved one passes, they stay around us. There are moments where you will see, feel or smell something that makes you think of them. My Nanna and Grandad passed some years ago. I have a photo of them both pinned to a corkboard in my kitchen. This photo shows my Nanna firmly hugging my Grandad and captures her soul at that very moment. You can see the enormous amount of true love she felt for him pouring out from this image. There are days when I walk into my kitchen and this photo will somehow be lying in the middle of the kitchen floor. Quite amazing considering how firmly it was pinned to the corkboard.

This happens at my sister's house too. Nanna was strong, kind, loving and gentle. Nothing meant more to her than her family. Her children and grandchildren were precious, and I will always be grateful for having had her as my grandmother. Her warm, loving, beautiful face is still etched on all of our hearts to this day. Even though she has passed, I still feel the same sense of warmth come over me when I look at her photo.

I feel sad for the many who miss the signs from their passed-on loved ones reassuring them that they are still around. It's even sadder for those who find it difficult to acknowledge the passing of their loved ones. The sadness is often so overwhelming that it stops them from remembering the treasured memories they shared. It was never more evident to me than now that my Virgo male's years of never speaking about his father's passing were just his way of protecting himself from the sadness he had felt when he lost him. I realised that over the years he too had missed the signs that, although his father is not with him physically, he has remained not far from him spiritually. We spent some hours talking about Ted that evening under the moonlight glow.

Acknowledging the loss of my Virgo male's anchor was definitely therapeutic and helped ease the pain and sadness that comes with losing a loved one. We both felt like Ted was with us on that balcony, ensuring that we could feel his love surrounding us. That night, when we finally moved inside, I saw my Virgo male staring at a photo of his dear dad.

The energy we had experienced under the moonlight and in front of the candle really affected us both. We knew that we were well and truly overdue for a change, and we were both ready to write a new chapter in our lives. My Virgo male acknowledged that his dad would have wanted him to live the best life possible without fear and anxiety. Sometimes a scent will remind you of a loved one who has passed. You may even hear a song that brings back a special moment that you shared with this person. Whenever you think of them, they are never too far away.

I remember when our son was six and he ran his very first race at his school sports day. My Junior Virgo male was not that enthusiastic about school sports. He was, however, particularly fond of his PlayStation. When he woke up on sports day and I came tearing into his room wearing his school house colours singing, "Red fans in the stands, stand up and SHOUT IT! Red team's gonna win, no doubt about it. GO RED!" the colour drained from his face. He proceeded to fake a stomach-ache to avoid going to school. Initially, I really thought my Junior Virgo male was ill. Over the years I have learnt the hard way that my Junior Virgo male is actually a very good actor, and if he wanted to, he could certainly pursue a career on *Grey's Anatomy* or some other medical soap opera.

Clearly, I was disappointed that he was too ill to attend sports day because I was pumped and ready for the occasion. When I informed Junior Virgo male that he would clearly have to rest and recover, the colour magically returned to his face and he snuggled up on the couch and settled down for a relaxing day of playing on the PlayStation. His stomach-ache seemed to stop. He ordered hot chocolate and toast, and I knew instantly that I had been duped. His award-winning performance had won him freedom from participating in sports day.

I had been up since 5.30am, preparing a picnic for myself and my parents to enjoy with my Junior Virgo male at the event. I had carefully selected my red outfit to show my support for my son's team, and I was pleased that my attire represented a united front as well as good taste in casual fashion! I had red streamers, red cupcakes, and red fingernails.

My Junior Virgo male wasn't particularly athletic, nor was he a fast runner, but he was really good at playing the game "Dance Revolution" on PlayStation, and obviously that was more appealing than running around the oval at school on sports day with his mother chanting, "You can do it!"

As I retreated to the kitchen to get my Junior Virgo male some breakfast, I heard music coming from the lounge room. He had suddenly recuperated and was now break dancing in front of the television. Shocked at how quickly he had recovered and furious that he had pulled the wool over my eyes yet again to avoid participating in his first school sports day, I turned off the television and advised him to go get ready for school immediately. Sheepishly, he retreated to his room and got dressed.

He tried one more time to collapse on the floor, clutching his stomach, but my Medusa-like expression was enough for him to grab his school bag and hide behind my parents, who were clearly able to protect him from turning to stone.

My Junior Virgo male was a particularly cute little boy. He had beautiful blonde hair, sparkling blue eyes and an infectious, cheeky smile that would melt any heart even when he had pushed you to the limits. When I was cross with him, he would snuggle into me and tell me that he loved me, and with that, the turmoil and disruption caused by his mischievous behaviour would be forgotten.

We headed to sports day. The school oval was ablaze with colour and excitement. I was so thrilled to be sharing his first sports day with my parents, who were visiting from Western Australia. We settled in under a huge Eucalypt tree with other families, and the roar of the teams' chanting created an electric atmosphere. All the grade one students were scheduled to compete in their races first. They were more likely to get tired quickly, and their attention spans were limited to say the least, so it was vital to get them racing at their peak. My Junior Virgo male was scheduled to race at 10am.

I watched him line up with his competitors. Standing at the starting line, his goal was to run 100 metres as fast as he could. Obviously, coming first and winning was the ultimate goal, and the first six-year-old across the finish line would receive a shiny gold ribbon. Mum, Dad and I went down to the sidelines so we could get a good view of the event.

CHAPTER SIX

I glanced over at the children preparing to race. I could see my darling Junior Virgo male commando rolling across the lawn. He would jump up and fall into a ninja stance whilst eyeballing his six-year-old competitors, and then he would high five them and pull back into another ninja stance. For a moment, I thought he was using these ninja elements to psych out his competitors. As I watched him pull up into a warrior pose and then fall down onto the ground and do the worm, I realised that the Jackie Chan movie he watched the weekend prior to the event and the "Dance Revolution" game he had been playing were actually the influencing factors here, and there was absolutely no focus at all on the fact that he was about to compete in a race.

The children were told to get ready, and they all stood very still. "On your marks! Get set! Go!" The gun was fired, signifying the beginning of the race. All the children started running, and all of the parents stood on the sidelines, cheering their babies on. You could see that there were parents who were expecting their offspring to win the ribbon, and then there were the parents who were just thrilled to see their kids having fun and participating. I was just happy for my Junior Virgo male to compete. As long as he finished the race, life would be sweet, even if I had to run behind him, encouraging him to experience the thrill of starting and finishing something no matter how hard the journey in-between.

I am pleased to say that most of the children were running forward. They were all neck and neck for the first few minutes, and then slowly some of the leaner, more athletic children started to surge forward, and their parents' screams and words of encouragement got louder and louder. I could see my Junior Virgo male, bless him, running slowly down the back of the pack. He was positioned nicely at second last, so we were happy with that. At least he wasn't last! After the morning's performance to avoid participation, we knew it was highly likely that he was going to end up in Hollywood and not at the Olympics, so it was all good!

As the children got halfway round the track, some of the front runners started to lose steam and fall slightly behind. Suddenly, my Junior Virgo male picked up speed. His little legs went into overdrive, his arms were pushing through the wind, and he just surged ahead. He swiftly passed all of his competitors. My Junior Virgo male took the lead!

I clutched my heart and grabbed hold of Mum, who was screaming and jumping up and down with sheer delight. My dad ran up to the finish line so my Junior Virgo male could see him. Dad wanted to be the first one to congratulate him for his efforts. I was slightly hysterical as my Junior Virgo male ran past us and gave us the big thumbs-up. I couldn't believe he was about to win the race. Who would have thought?

He was in the lead and just two meters from the finish line when, out of the blue, I heard a familiar hearty belly laugh. I stopped for a moment as I was slightly confused. I knew this laugh. It was a distinctive roar of love and laughter combined. It sounded like it came from someone standing right behind me, but there simply wasn't anyone aside from Mum within close proximity. I said to my mum, "Did you hear that laughter?" She said, "No." I said to her that it had sounded just like Ted's laugh.

I was sure I had heard my father-in-law's laugh at that moment. I heard it as clear as day. It was as if he were by my side, watching what was happening. I truly felt, from the bottom of my heart, after hearing that laughter that he was with us in spirit, watching his grandson win his first race. I tried to make sense of it. Perhaps I had imagined it? Maybe

I had just heard someone else laughing. In my mind, though, there was no mistaking this laugh.

Within a few seconds of hearing this joyous roar, my son crossed the finish line and won the race. I have no doubt that my father-in-law shared this special moment with us, and somehow he made me aware of his presence in his own special way. I am so glad I didn't miss this sign as it just reminded me that he is always watching over his grandson.

> *"In the midst of movement and chaos,*
> *keep stillness inside of you."*
> —**Deepak Chopra M.D.**

CHAPTER SEVEN

Procrastination: It's a Curse

My Virgo male and I awoke early one Sunday morning, and we decided to head down to one of our beautiful Northern beaches for a coffee. The beaches in North Queensland are very tropical: coconut palms line the foreshores, the sand is soft and white, and the warm waters of the Pacific Ocean lap at your feet. It's quite scenic and very pleasant except for the odd sign that says: Beware! Crocodiles and box jellyfish inhabit these waters!

We strolled along the boardwalk. I rarely venture near the water's edge for obvious reasons. We stopped and gazed out towards the horizon. The sun shone down through the clouds, and the turquoise sea sparkled and glimmered. It's not often we stop and acknowledge how precious life is, but this was definitely one of those breathtaking moments where we simply had to appreciate how wonderful the world really is!

Once again, we both felt forced to stop and take it all in. It was as if someone was standing behind us, ensuring we received the message that it is important to slow down and really be grateful for every single day. I often remind myself that if this were my last day on earth, would anyone really care what I weighed, what I wore or how big my house was? I have often asked this same question to some of my close friends when their lives have been in turmoil. It's quite confronting

The Shed

when you ask yourself that question. It makes you stop and re-evaluate what really counts.

If this was my last day on earth, I would want to ensure that I had told my family and friends that I loved them. I would want to make sure that I was leaving this world knowing that my life had been filled with many precious moments rather than many precious items. I would want to appreciate and hold on tight to all that I hold closest to my heart right to the very end.

It really was a special morning, and we soaked up the calmness that had completely overtaken both of us. We enjoyed coffee at a beach-side café and then decided to head home as my Virgo male said he had things he wanted to do around our house. While driving home, I got the uncontrollable urge to bring up the old shed yet again. I tried desperately to swallow the words that were now surging upwards in my throat. I had kept them suppressed for as long as I could. It was as if I had no control over my own thoughts, or my mouth for that matter, as the following question rolled off my tongue: "I don't suppose you are going to clean out the shed? It's really about time you did that, you know. We have had enough signs now to know that it's something that needs addressing." I had certainly kept that bottled up for a while!

My Virgo male didn't respond. His stony silence indicated that he was still resisting the challenge that would accompany this task. We arrived home, and we both started working in the garden. I went to clean the pool located out back, and my Virgo male went to the front of the house. He had been really quiet all morning. After a while, I wandered around the front to see what he was doing. My Virgo male was hovering near the shed. I pretended I was putting something in the bin and

CHAPTER SEVEN

said, "What are you doing?" He replied, "Oh, just cleaning up a bit."

My throat was so tight that it hurt. I wanted to scream, "For goodness' sake, clean that shed up!" Once again, the shed-cleaning situation had resurfaced. *Clean the shed, clean the shed!* It was like a relentless voice in my head that would not stop repeating the message. Until he did it, I would not get any peace.

I walked away from him and went back to the pool. After about 20 minutes, my Virgo male came around the back of the house, holding a saw.

Obviously, he was about to cut down some foliage. If you could see our yard, which is overgrown with tropical plants and trees, you would realise that his efforts would really not even make a dent in the area. In fact, the beauty lies within its wildness and lushness, but clearly my Virgo male was trying to avoid doing the inevitable. After a few minutes of cutting down branches, he dropped the saw and disappeared. I did the old 'head to the bin with pretend rubbish' trick to see where he had gone. He was standing at the shed doors, staring inside. I wanted to scream, "JUST DO IT!" but I bit my tongue and walked away.

It must have been an overwhelming experience for him to stand and look inside the shed. You see, it was not only the mess that he was confronting—it was so much more. I returned to the pool. I thought after about 15 minutes of not seeing him that he must have finally stepped inside and begun this almighty mission, but I turned around and saw him coming towards me with a pair of hedge clippers.

Once again, he had walked away from a situation that he felt overwhelmed by. As he walked towards me, we both stopped and faced each other. Locked in our own private battles, we stared deeply into each other's eyes, pool scoop in my hand and hedge clippers in his. We were close enough to start a war, and we were both well and truly armed for battle. It was clearly time to sort out this shed.

Stifling the words for long enough, I looked directly into his eyes and said, "The shed is a mess. We have had some uncanny warnings about cleaning it up. It seems like the universe is giving you the opportunity to sort through a lot of clutter and unfinished business. When all this is done, you will feel better and you will be able to move forward. It's time you cleaned out your shed."

My Virgo male stood for a moment and stared back at me intensely. After a minute, he put the clippers down on the deck, almost like he was surrendering his weapon, and he turned around and walked away. I stood frozen. I couldn't move. I felt overwhelmed with emotion, but then something made me look up from the pool deck towards the top storey of our house.

For a brief second, I saw the silhouette of a man staring out from our kitchen window. There was no one home—no one inside—so I was a little taken aback. I wasn't scared or shocked when I saw this large figure looking down at me, however, because he was familiar. Although it was only a moment, I realised I was getting another brief glimpse of my father-in-law. Once again, I was certain he was letting me know that he was around us in good times and in challenging times.

> *"Whatever the mind of man can conceive and believe, it can achieve."*
> —**Napoleon Hill**

CHAPTER EIGHT
And the Healing has Begun

Finally, my Virgo male had also realised that there was definitely something far more significant occurring than just his beloved wife's need for organisation in the shed. The task of clearing out the past was very much confronting him. It had become apparent to both of us that the job at hand was more about symbolism than tidiness!

I knew I had to stay away from him whilst he sorted through some very personal memories and items that were gathered in the shed. I also acknowledged that this cleaning was one task that my Virgo male had to complete on his own. He knew it too, and finally it was time to stop ignoring the obvious and tackle the mess.

Two hours had passed, and I had not seen or heard a sound from my Virgo male. I simply had to go check on what was happening. I walked around the side of our home, about 10 metres from the shed. I could see my Virgo male inside, shirt off and head down, deep in thought and surrounded by clutter.

His Ute, which was parked next to the shed, was already piled high with items and rubbish. I desperately wanted to go take a peak and see what it was like inside, but I felt like something was pulling me back from intruding into this clean-up. I was getting much better at listening to my own intuition, so I retreated and walked away.

The dreaded shed! It stored so many things all in one place.

From my perspective, symbolically, it was becoming evident that the shed now resembled the mind and the heart. We often hold on to bad memories and rehash over incomplete goals. We see these experiences as failures. We keep them all locked away deep down inside, but we find these experiences keep resurfacing, creating uncertainty, frustration, insecurity and chaos in our lives. Being overwhelmed with confusion and lack of clarity becomes a way of life because nothing is ever cleared out, removed and acknowledged.

You cannot learn from life's experiences without stopping and acknowledging why it is that sometimes things become fractured and broken. You have to decide if you can fix or repair the damage to move forward. If not repairable, acknowledge this and then grow and learn from the experience. If there is any guilt associated with it, discard it quickly. Guilt is a completely wasted emotion, so release it and free up space for more uplifting, pleasurable feelings!

My Virgo male was staring directly at many of his past experiences in the shed. He had managed to keep some kind of memento from every single adventure, the good ones and the bad ones. The symbolism of cleaning out the shed was also becoming very evident for my Virgo male. Without acknowledging our negative experiences or past mistakes, we often store them layer upon layer in our minds and our hearts, leaving little room for growth.

How many times have you started something and never completed the job? You put the project away in a safe place and vow to get back to it, but it never happens. When confronted with the incompletion, you experience feelings of regret and disappointment.

How many times have you held on to something that a person from your past has given you? Perhaps it is jewellery

CHAPTER EIGHT

from a relationship that ended badly. That jewellery is a constant reminder of the hurt, sadness and often bitterness experienced from that time in your life. Rarely do we focus on the joy that may have been associated with that time.

How many times have you walked into your office to find that it is piled high with bills that need paying, receipts that need filing, and work that needs addressing? It gets unbelievably overwhelming each day as it grows more and more out of control. Not prioritising it all creates endless stress.

Why do some of us keep broken computers, broken phones, and broken TVs? We insist that we will use them again, but rarely do we get around to fixing them. Why do we not just pass them on to someone who can repair them? Many of us keep mountains of useless items, creating visual and mental clutter.

'Out of sight, out of mind' is really not the best solution when it comes to life's messes. They always manage to resurface. My Virgo male was in that shed for nine hours that Sunday. His Ute overflowed with items that symbolised many memories, ideas and projects started but never completed. Each item symbolised incompletion in some way. This incompletion was due to the fact that the source of support my Virgo male once had was now gone. Most of us have a special someone whom we talk to when we need words of advice and encouragement. That person is solid and wise and gives you just the right dose of sympathy and encouragement as well as the push you need in the right direction to go the distance. My Virgo male's dad had been his voice of reason and encouragement.

This was no ordinary shed clean-up. This clean-up was about refocusing and finding that power within—the power that makes you completely confident in all of your own decisions in life, whether they are right or wrong. If they are wrong, you are strong enough to accept and grow from the lesson. The shed clean-up was also about letting go of the past, acknowledging it, and moving forward to face the future. It was about seeing our way forward without obstructions and distractions. It was about having faith and confidence in our own abilities. It was about trusting our own judgment and making decisions wholeheartedly from our own innerstrength. The biggest message of all from the shed clean-up was that sometimes we have to take a step backwards and do a bit of clearing out in order to go forward.

Finally, my Virgo male walked out of the shed. I now felt comfortable in going over to him. I said, "Are you ok?" and he replied, "Yes, I believe I am. I feel clearer. There are a lot of memories in the back of my Ute. Not many of those memories hold positive experiences, but somehow I feel like I am about to lay all of that to rest."

It was like a huge weight had been lifted from my Virgo male's shoulders. It certainly had been a therapeutic experience for him, and this was definitely no ordinary shed clean-up. He continued to explain that he was feeling really relieved, clearer and much more focused. He said that when he now looked inside the shed and could see his tools and special items clearly without distraction, he felt like he was able to focus and plan a more solid future. He was also feeling a great deal of satisfaction because he had started the clean-up, followed it through and completed the job. He felt totally motivated to go forward and start a fresh new day with a clean slate.

I too looked inside the shed. The once dishevelled mess was now organised. All the building tools were carefully placed to one side. Our son's skateboard and scooter were now easily

CHAPTER EIGHT

accessible and visible. These items symbolised our gorgeous boy's vibrant, energetic childhood. I remember we had taken a vacation to Hawaii when my Virgo Junior male was nine. He scooted all over Honolulu on his little silver scooter with us. It was a wonderful memory.

Two fishing rods remained in the shed. My Virgo male loved to fish. His dear dad had taught both his sons how to catch the elusive 'big one'. My Virgo male rarely took the time to enjoy fishing anymore. These two rods clearly represented that it was time he cast out another line and take some time out to relax in a peaceful environment. My Virgo male has always found calm when he is around water.

There was a huge space right in the centre of the shed and as I stood in it, I felt clear and in control. It's amazing what a good clean-up will do! My Virgo male jumped into his Ute and said, "Well, this whole shed clean-up won't be completed until I dump all this stuff," and with that he drove off and headed to the rubbish disposal to take a load off, so to speak!

About one hour later, my Virgo male arrived back home with an empty Ute. He came upstairs, showered, poured me a glass of red wine and then opened an ice-cold beer and sat with me on our deck. He took a big deep breath and then said "Cheers!" He was calmer than I had ever seen him before. With all the mess that had created so much darkness and heaviness now removed, the light was certainly able to start shining through.

"Beautiful light is born of darkness, so the faith that springs from conflict is often the strongest and the best."
— **R. Turnbull**

CHAPTER NINE
The Symbolic Shed and its Message

We have all experienced life's ups and downs. The challenges that we often face can be overwhelming. Life is a continuous journey of highs and lows, and if we don't experience the lows, we are unable to appreciate the energy of the highs. As difficult as it is, experiencing hardship or hurt allows us to learn valuable lessons.

It's normal to feel unsure about what direction we should take in life. Fear and uncertainty are emotions commonly associated with change. These emotions often shake up our confidence and make us retreat rather than go forward. Fear is a distressing negative sensation induced by a perceived threat. In short, when it comes to fear, you can flee from it or confront it.

Any new opportunity that is presented to us in life is normally accompanied by some fear. Uncertainty and contemplation go hand in hand when faced with something that challenges us. Sadly, this negative emotion can stop us from reaching our full potential and experiencing the growth that comes from working through life's challenges. With or without the happy ending, all of life's experiences can be viewed with optimism.

I remember when I was pregnant with my Junior Virgo male. I was well and truly overdue. The doctor had decided that if I had not gone into labour by Monday morning, they would induce it. On Sunday afternoon, I was at Mum and Dad's house. They have this great space in the front of their home. My family refers to it as 'the front room'. With all due respect, creativity with names has never been our family's strength!

It is a big warm, sunny room with lovely gold velvet lounge chairs that are really comfortable to sit on and beautiful gold silk curtains that cascade down the sides of the huge floor to ceiling windows that encase the room. It gives a perfect view of the picturesque street outside. In a nutshell, it is a very heart-warming space.

The sun always seems to shine right into this room and send in lots of warmth and energy, and the room is filled with a lifetime of emotions and experiences. We have often all gathered in the front room and laughed, cried and shared many special moments. Words of wisdom and encouragement have been shared along with copious amounts of tea. There have been countless times that family and friends have all sat together in this space, discussing life's problems.

We are all naturally drawn together in this room, and it is the foundation from which we support one another and encourage each other to go the distance, no matter what the challenge. After you have shared your concerns with the family in this space, you can clearly see your way forward.

On this particular Sunday afternoon, I was sitting in one of the gorgeous gold chairs. I was so heavily pregnant that I could hardly get up. Mum had made my sister and me some tea, and we were discussing the impending arrival of our Junior Virgo male. Mum was saying, "Well, this time tomorrow, you will have that beautiful baby boy in your arms". When my mum said those words, I felt this overwhelming sense of uncertainty completely take over my body. I started to cry. Mum quickly came to me and wrapped her arms around me. That in itself was quite difficult because I was enormous! She said, "Don't worry; you will be fine. They will give you something if you can't cope with the contractions. Once you get that baby in your arms, you will forget about the pain". I was now sobbing uncontrollably. It wasn't the pain I was scared of; I was terrified about becoming a mum. What if I dropped him? What if I left him in the supermarket? What if the whole mothering thing didn't come naturally to me?

In this instance, I actually had no choice in whether or not to flee or confront my current fear. My mum put it quite simply, "Well, darling, that baby is coming into this world whether you like it or not!" Mum also reassured me that I would make a fabulous mother and that she was always just a phone call away if I needed help. I was nervous to say the least, but fortunately, this was one event where the anxiety quickly faded and was superseded by the power of love.

The shed symbolises the many opportunities and experiences that had been presented to my Virgo male. Inside were unfinished projects that were always started and never completed because of the anxiety that accompanies the unknown. Each project started would begin with the promise of good things to come. The further into each project, the harder it became to finish the task. Fear of failure would often take over, and the project would be put on the back burner (or in our case, in the shed) for another day.

The shed also reflects the huge hole left in my Virgo male's heart at no longer having his father available for that Sunday afternoon talk over a beer. This was the very special talk that always picked him up and motivated him to succeed and trust in himself. We should never take for granted those precious moments that we share with our loved ones.

Imagine you are walking down a pathway and you are not sure what you will encounter at the end of that path. It's a long, hilly pathway that is challenging and takes your breath away. You get halfway down the path, and you are exhausted. You stop and turn back, never completing the journey, because you are apprehensive that you will not make it to the end. It's easier to stop.

The shed symbolises the many emotions that we feel as we travel down life's path. It's the representation of constant beginnings with no ends. It represents the overwhelming feelings that we experience when we are consumed with life's demands and are unable to move forward, causing us to retreat.

Looking inside the shed, you could see the fractured, cluttered pieces from years gone by all thrown in together. Visually overwhelming and emotionally daunting, this area had become so overloaded that there was little room left for anything else.

What does the big cleaning up of our shed symbolise? It symbolises clarity, acknowledgement, lessons, growth and space for new beginnings. It is also a reminder to keep a firm grip on what you are doing daily to ensure that life does not spiral out of control. A lifetime of lessons has emerged from that one tiny shed. These lessons are so valuable that the journey to learn them was worth it.

Our run of bad luck had not been caused by a curse or our messy shed's location. It was just a testing time when circumstances were not going in our favour. Our run of bad luck and our messages from the enlightened ones did, however, lead us to cleaning up the shed, and that in itself has brought home to us the importance of being clear-minded, organised and open-hearted so we are ready for whatever life throws at us.

We all need support and guidance, but if you do not have someone to support you in this way, it is important to listen and trust your own inner-voice. Your inner-voice is your intuition, and it will never let you down. Just be sure that you can hear it!

> *"Just because you failed yesterday or all day today,*
> *or a moment ago, all that matters is:*
> *What are you going to do, right now?"*
> — **Author unknown**

CHAPTER TEN

Honey, Don't Walk that Dog

Trusting your own intuition takes strength. The word 'intuition' comes from the Latin word 'intueri', which is often roughly translated as meaning 'to look inside'. In simple terms, intuition is that gut feeling that something is either right or wrong. Often it comes through your body as a feeling or emotion. Sometimes it is a thought. It is that inner-voice that you seem to hear over and over again, eventually becoming too loud to ignore. If you are having trouble hearing, feeling or trusting your intuition, then perhaps it's time to clear out what is causing the blockage.

Over the last few years, I have made it a priority to develop my own intuition and trust it completely. It has certainly taken me some time to develop it and some hard lessons have been learnt in the process. We are all constantly reminded of women's intuition, but let's make no mistake here: men have just as much intuition as women. I think women are often more open to trusting their feelings whereas some men are conditioned to keep their feelings and emotions locked away.

Men often respond to situations differently to women. They often have the ability to look at things and base a choice on rationality, but rationality is not always the right basis for a decision.

I think of the many times I have ignored my intuition as it screamed out a massive warning to me. Every time I ignored it, the situation turned out to be less than favourable. I should have paid close attention to my inner-voice some years ago when my Virgo male and I were offered a contract to undertake a position managing a tropical island resort.

It seemed like a fabulous opportunity. The resort had never been taken to its full potential as a holiday destination, and we were approached to be the team to make it a tourist hot spot. Along with the great working contract on offer, we were enticed by palm trees, free meals created for us by an award-winning chef, gorgeous accommodation for us to reside in and sunshine every day of the year! Sounds too good to be true, doesn't it?

When we met the owner of this fantastic resort, he was charming and funny. He wined and dined with us and promised us a long and prosperous career. He assured us that we would have free reign when it came to decision-making while we transformed this quiet island accommodation into a world-class retreat! My Virgo male and I had a reputation for transforming holiday accommodations into thriving properties. It was our specialty, and we were keen for a change as well as a challenge, so the timing was impeccable.

We had a lovely dinner with the owner, and as we sat in this spectacular location deciding whether or not we would accept his employment proposal, I couldn't help but experience this nagging feeling that something wasn't quite right. For every positive my Virgo male pointed out, I would quickly bring up a negative. I can still see us sitting on the veranda of this majestic resort. It was a full moon, and we were overlooking a spectacular swimming pool. This resort had tremendous room for improvement and was ideal for weddings, honeymooners and families alike who wanted an exotic holiday destination. We simply could not ignore its potential.

CHAPTER TEN

My Virgo male was excited by the challenge, and I was keen, but my inner-voice was still screaming that something was not quite right. I insisted we travel back home before we made a final decision on this offer, but I could see my Virgo male was good to go on the project. I did feel somewhat guilty about being so negative about the whole scenario because it all appeared so promising. I rarely shy away from a challenge or an opportunity that will bring satisfaction, but I still felt really uneasy about this one.

As we boarded the ferry to return us to the mainland, we could not ignore the island's beauty. It was a fantastic, sunny day. The waters surrounding the island were crystal clear and turquoise blue. The promise of an exciting job opportunity was certainly enticing. The resort owner shook our hands on departure. He reiterated that he would eagerly await our decision and looked forward to the possibility of having us take his business to a new level.

As the boat pulled away from the island, I could feel my Virgo male's energy. He was so excited at this new prospect and its location. It was overwhelming! He kept reminding me of what an unbelievable opportunity it would be for us. I looked back at the beautiful island as the ferry horn sounded, and I had this sinking feeling that we just shouldn't do it. There was nothing untoward or questionable relating to it, but it just felt wrong. I will never forget that as we pulled away from the jetty, I could just hear in my head, "Warning, warning! This is all wrong! Just say NO!"

On returning home, we realised that we had to make a quick decision on this contract. We had to discuss whether we would accept or decline the opportunity as soon as possible. As my Virgo male was so enthusiastic about it and there was no evidence of any negativity in relation to the contract except for my inner-voice, which was now screaming at me, we decided to accept the position. I can still remember saying reluctantly, "OK, I will do it."

Whilst everyone around us was green with envy and toasting our success, I still had a bad feeling associated with the contract. I couldn't put my finger on it, but it felt all wrong. Everyone reminded me that I was probably just feeling nervous about the move away from family and friends and obviously the concern of finding a new school for my Junior Virgo male was an influencing factor. They all reassured me that once I settled into this new role, everything would be fine! Not convinced, I packed us up and reluctantly took on this new challenge regardless of the sinking feeling in my stomach.

We were due to commence our management positions on Monday, but we decided to get to the island on the Wednesday before that so we could have a few days to settle in. We arrived at the island resort at around 9pm, expecting to be greeted by the resort owner. After all, he had informed us that he would be awaiting our arrival. Our new employer usually resided in Tasmania, but he would always spend a portion of each month at the resort, ensuring everything was in order. He had explained to us that after we were settled into our new management roles, he would prefer to limit his visits and leave us to control the running of the property so he could spend more time with his family.

We walked into the magnificent reception area of the resort, and instead of being greeted by the resort owner we were met by a very irritable woman. She was rude and extremely unwelcoming. She directed us to a nearby villa and informed us that our manager's apartment had not been cleaned for our arrival but it would be done over the weekend. When she

CHAPTER TEN

left us alone, I said to my Virgo male, "Well, that's not how we want our guests to be greeted! First impressions count! Obviously a little customer service training is called for here. If she is unable to be more welcoming, she will simply have to be directed to another role!" I added that to the top of my to-do list. The highest priority would be given to finding her a role that gave her satisfaction. Clearly, the job she was doing now was making her miserable. Was I in for a rude shock!

We had a few days to unwind and get familiar with the surroundings, but even in the first instance, there were signs emerging that all was not as it seemed. We were informed that our manager's accommodation was now available for us to move into. Originally, we had been shown a beautiful apartment, but now we were being directed to a dilapidated old duplex. Our original welcoming party escorted us up to our new home. I will refer to her as Little Miss Grumpy as it is certainly an accurate assessment of her demeanour. As we approached, we noticed a vicious dog in the courtyard, guarding the old, clapped-out building. The dog was snarling at us and was frothing at the mouth. Little Miss Grumpy screamed at the dog, "Shut up!" and then she bent down and started kissing and petting the beast!

I demanded that Little Miss Grumpy explain to me what was going on. What had happened to our lovely apartment, and who owned this frightening wild dog? Sternly, Little Miss Grumpy informed me that my Virgo male and I would have the first duplex and she resided right next door in the second duplex. We would be sharing everything with her, including the veranda, the garden, the laundry and the dog! The dog was her baby. Don't get me wrong—I like dogs, but this one terrified me.

It was evident that Little Miss Grumpy was annoyed at

our arrival at the resort because she had been using the first duplex, our new home, for storage and she had full run of the property. By now, the warning that I had been hearing in my head was sounding like the siren that is sounded over the radio when a natural disaster is about to occur. It's the alarm that the government uses to warn all residents of impending doom: a "Whoooop, Whoooop" sound followed by an urgent voice saying, "Warning, warning!" It conjures up feelings of panic and the urgency to run to safer ground. That same alarm is often sounded in naval war movies when a torpedo is about to hit!

Within 24 hours of meeting Little Miss Grumpy, we realised that we really should have paid more attention to my overwhelming feeling that something wasn't right. To summarise our island adventure, we found out the hard way that Little Miss Grumpy was the boss's mistress. He would visit his island resort and stay for a while, and she would ensure that his every need was met—and I do mean his every need!

This resort was their little hideaway. He had promised her that he would eventually leave his wife and sell the resort. They would move overseas and live happily ever after. She was obviously a little discontented that he had not fulfilled his promise to her and was getting rather cranky waiting for him to do so. She was now concerned that if we improved the resort and made it successful, he would never sell it. She made it very clear that we were not welcome. Her intention was to wreak enormous havoc, making it virtually impossible for us to succeed with our goal of improving the property.

After dealing with endless troublesome scenarios caused by Little Miss Grumpy, we informed Mr Boss-man that we would stay on and run the resort on the condition that Little Miss

CHAPTER TEN

Grumpy was either removed or advised of the importance of allowing us to fulfil our obligations as managers. We were keen to find an amicable solution so we could complete our task. He said that he was purchasing a property for her to reside in elsewhere on the island and if we could just hang on for a few weeks, all would be resolved.

Week after week, we were promised she would be relocated, and it never happened. She was rude and nasty to everyone she encountered. Staff and guests alike were showered with abuse from her. She attempted to ensure that everyone's experience at the resort was one to remember for all the wrong reasons!

The final straw came when Mr Boss-man arrived for his monthly meeting. He told us that he was going to pack up Little Miss Grumpy's belongings and remove her from the resort immediately. He knew how destructively she was behaving. An hour later, our head housekeeper came running into my office in tears. When asked what was wrong, she informed me that she had just ventured into a vacated hotel room to service it. She had knocked, but there had been no response. She opened the door only to be confronted with Little Miss Grumpy and Mr Boss-man in a compromising situation. She was completely embarrassed and visibly shocked at what she had seen.

Little Miss Grumpy had informed our head housekeeper that she would no longer be employed if she revealed the illicit affair. That was the final straw for us! We packed our bags and left the very next day. What is the moral of our island adventure? We should really have listened to my intuition's warnings of trouble in paradise!

Another example of trusting your intuition became apparent recently when a dear friend of mine separated from her partner. He had captured her heart with his charming ways, and this beautiful girl was smitten. She quickly fell in love with this man and was looking forward to a future with him. After their separation, she was very upset. Often when the sadness kicks in, you tend to remember only the good times. The negative part of the relationship fades as the loneliness becomes all-consuming.

Even though she knew deep down in her heart that she had done the right thing by separating from him, she still had a deep connection with this man despite his faults. During the initial separation, he continued contacting her in the hope that they would reconnect. He played on her kind, sympathetic nature by trying to get her to feel sorry for him.

As an outsider looking in at this situation, it was very easy for me to see what he was doing. As a friend, I gave her a gentle warning of what he was up to. She was still connected to him emotionally, however, and slowly but surely he was enticing her back into his world.

While they were together, they had a lovely pet dog. They were both terribly fond of their little Poochie. Their dog was unlike Little Miss Grumpy's dog. It was much gentler and definitely not trained to kill! After the break up, the ex-lover started to contact my dear friend, asking her to come over and take their little dog for a walk. He had explained that he was just too unwell to take Poochie for his morning run. He knew she would consider it because she loved that dog and he made her feel too guilty not to do it! By enticing her into walking the dog, he was able to slowly work on weakening her defences, enabling him to slide back into her world. Contacting her and asking her to take the dog for a walk enabled that connection to continue. Little by little, his 'poor me and poor Poochie' scenario, as weak as it was, would strengthen his connection with her.

Feeling really obliged by his requests, she decided to walk Poochie on one occasion, even though I had warned her, "Honey, don't walk that dog!" It was obvious what he was doing. She had to see her ex to pick up Poochie for his walk, and he would then declare that he was unable to live without her. At the same time, little Poochie would be crying at her feet. She would be toast!

After that first walk, I could see she was having second thoughts about their relationship. Her ex-boyfriend too could see she was weakening, and he tried again. "Please take Poochie for another walk. I am just far too sick to do it." Again, I warned her, "Honey, don't walk that dog!"

Whilst she was feeling confused and torn apart by it all, I offered her the following advice, "Put your hand on your heart and ask yourself, 'Do I love this man? Is he being honest and forthright with me? Is he the right one?' Then, stop and be silent. Listen for the answer. The first answer you feel or hear will be your intuition giving you the right advice." She did just that and informed me later that, when she put her hand on her heart, she knew instantly that he was not right for her. From then on she started to disconnect herself from him.

About a week later, she was down at the beach and was about to grab coffee from what was once her and her ex-boyfriend's favourite restaurant. It was their special place, the place where they had fallen in love. Just before she walked inside, she casually glanced over at their usual table. They had claimed this table as their own because it was quiet, romantic and had a beautiful view.

What she saw at this table only reaffirmed that she had definitely made the right decision. She was confronted with her ex-boyfriend and another woman enjoying a very flirtatious liaison. Clearly, he was too unwell to walk their dog but not unwell enough that he couldn't behave like one! Luckily for her, this time around she had listened to her inner-voice. She did not like what it had to say, but it saved her from a lifetime of heartache.

Don't ever doubt your intuition, your inner-voice, or your gut instinct. If you are unsure, put your hand on your heart and ask the questions you need answered. What you hear and feel is all that you need to acknowledge. Trust the answer you get. It will rarely lead you down the wrong path, but ignoring it often will.

Take steps every day to clean up all the unnecessary mind clutter so you can be sure to hear that inner-voice loud and clear!

"Cease trying to work everything out with your minds. It will get you nowhere. Live by intuition and inspiration, and let your whole life be revelation."
—**Eileen Caddy**

CHAPTER ELEVEN

The Rhythm of Life: Can You Feel it?

Life has a rhythm, and this rhythm consists of beats and time. Our daily life consists of these continuous beats and time. Everything we do—every activity we partake in and every situation we encounter—creates a moment. Ideally, these moments should flow freely with life's beat, but all too often, our lives are so overwhelming that we are unable to feel it.

There are just 24 hours in a day and seven days in a week. Do you feel like time is speeding up? When the beats become faster and the moments become too intense, it's easy to lose your rhythm. If your rhythm is a little off-beat, there is no time like the present to start managing the rate and sequence. Your life will flow freely if you do.

Life's rhythm has strong and weak elements. The strong elements are the positive, wonderful, joyous moments that we experience in our lives. The weak elements are the emotionally draining occurrences that we encounter. If you see it the other way around, then perhaps it is time you re-evaluated how you look at your life. It can be quite challenging to flow with life's rhythm every day, but it can be done.

It's easy to tell if you are out of sync with the rhythm of your life. If you are overwhelmed, stressed and irritable or if you feel like you just cannot cope with everything that is coming your way, then clearly you have lost your rhythm. If you feel calm, focused, at ease, happy and peaceful, then you are certainly in tune with life's beat.

The world is spinning around so fast that it is normal to lose your balance and your rhythm. When nothing flows, life is difficult. If you are feeling this way, simply stop. Gather your thoughts, take time to breathe deeply and slowly, and address why things are challenging. Identify and eliminate all the unnecessary distractions that are overloading you. This will free you up, giving you some precious time to get back in tune with all that is surrounding you.

Fatigue can make you unable to keep up with life's beat, so take some time out to rest and recharge. Stress can overwhelm you and consume your thoughts and energy. Life's noise can drown out your rhythm. Traffic and crowds can increase your anxiety levels. Over the course of your day, it's important to take the time to stop and centre yourself. Being still and silent and focusing on your breathing will allow you to pick up the beat again.

I spent many weekends at Scarborough Beach in Western Australia when I was growing up. Scarborough Beach is a great surfing spot. My friends and I would swim and body surf until we were exhausted. I was never a great swimmer, but I still managed to enjoy the experience as long as I did not lose my rhythm in the sea.

Before I would wade into the warm waters of the Indian Ocean, I would stand at the edge and assess the huge waves rolling in. My friends would just head straight into the surf, but I liked to prepare myself. I would wade in waist-deep and stop in order to get a feel for the current as well as the flow of the waves. I did not want to end up out of my depth. I would always notice the incredible shift in the tide and the almighty power of the swell building minute by minute. It was amazing

CHAPTER ELEVEN

to watch everyone in the water prepare and adapt to the waves breaking in their own special and yet unique way. Fear, excitement and joy—all these emotions were associated with the build up. When taking on one of these waves, there were many things to consider. The waves were big, and the current was fast. You had to be careful of rips, sharks, surfboards and other swimmers. If you didn't surf a wave in at just the right time, the massive wave forming behind the one you were considering catching would gather you up and then dump you. Being dumped is not a pleasant experience. You are spun around continuously, and you become completely helpless and out of control. Think of the spin cycle on your washing machine and imagine being in it!

As you are tumbling, if you open your eyes under the water, all you will see is sand, water and white wash, so it's best to keep your eyes closed. It feels like you will never surface from beneath the wave and all the while, you are running out of air. You struggle and hope to God that you will see the sun and catch a breath very soon.

If you were comfortable and confident in the surf, however, you would feel the big waves forming. The current would get faster, the surge would get stronger and you would know the wave was coming. Your gut instinct would tell you exactly when the right moment would be to swim with the wave. You could feel the water's flow building. If you were going with the flow, you would swiftly ride the wave back to shore. It would be exhilarating. The secret to catching a good wave is to feel, listen, trust and then 'go with the flow'.

Waves are a form of energy, which lifts water as it moves along. Behind the wave, the water rises and falls. Waves give rhythm to the ocean. The ocean itself is energy—natural energy—and the sound that comes from the waves breaking and crashing is the tremendous sound of the universe. Many of us have lost our sense of oneness with the universe. Getting dumped in the surf is similar to how you feel when your life is out of rhythm. Overall, it's frustrating, overwhelming and leaves you completely exhausted.

I am sure you have all heard the phrase, 'Go with the flow'. Going with the flow means accepting and moving through life's events with ease, confidence and clarity. In order for your life to flow smoothly, you really have to stay connected and grounded. Everything that happens in your life happens for a reason. Trusting in this belief will allow you the confidence to feel life's rhythm and bring you growth, peace and happiness.

Perhaps you have a lot of clutter surrounding you. Similar to what was in our shed, clutter blocks the flow of life's rhythm. Is there a lot of unnecessary noise inside your mind distracting and drowning out the rhythm of your life? Stop and identify what it is that is causing you to feel so out of control. Take the necessary steps to clear out and acknowledge all of the blockages. Take a minute to quiet down your mind. Eliminate some of that unnecessary mind noise. Ground yourself. Take time out and stand barefoot on the grass. Breathe deeply and connect with the earth. Connecting with the earth will allow you to feel relaxed, release anxiety and refocus.

In order to clear out your mind, you need to clear out your living and working spaces. Allow for some quiet time on a daily basis so you can gently tune back into life's rhythm. If you have forgotten the tune, you will quickly remember it when you take the necessary steps to allow the rhythm to flow back into your world.

Recently, I saw a friend on her morning walk. I was driving past her on my way to work. She had her headphones on connected to her iPod, and she was dancing down the street. Obviously, she was listening to a song that made her feel motivated enough to dance wildly—like no one was watching! Not only was she having a wow of a time but she was also spreading joy to everyone who passed her. I smiled and laughed at my vivacious friend dancing down our street, and the image of her shimmying her way to good health stayed with me all day.

Dancing is a wonderful way to release negative energy. It lifts the spirit instantly and is a great escape from life's overwhelming stresses. You don't have to do it publicly to benefit from the experience! When was the last time you danced? I dare you to put down this book, put on your favourite song and JUST DANCE. Forget about all of your cares and worries for a while. It will help you to get back into life's joyous rhythm. You will instantly feel uplifted! You will be amazed at how sweet the rhythm of life is when you can feel it! Experience the joy that comes from dancing in time with life's beat. Take positive steps every day to feel life's rhythm. Life is just too short not to dance! My mantra is to always 'live by the rhythm'. What's yours?

"Everything has rhythm, everything dances."
—**Maya Angelou**

CHAPTER TWELVE

Self-Esteem: Are You Running on Empty?

It is easy to lose your sense of self when you can't see your way forward. Remember that every day you are in complete control of your own life. You make the choices when it comes to how you will respond to your day's events. Of course, there will be challenges that test your patience and your resilience, but ultimately, how you react to them shows your inner strength.

When our self-esteem is low, it is often the case that we respond and view the world with a very negative outlook. There are many people suffering with low self-esteem, and they do a great job of bringing everyone around them down to their level. If you feel that your self-esteem has been depleted, don't waste another minute! Right now is the perfect time to top up your tank and start reminding yourself just how amazing you really are.

I gained a lot of weight when I was pregnant. I have always loved food. It nurtures us, energises us, entices us and is often the central focus of a celebration. While I was pregnant, I celebrated the opportunity to eat for two. After the birth of our baby son, I was resting in my hospital bed and I began chatting to another woman who was sharing my room. She had just given birth to her first child some eight hours before me. She was extremely confident and was taking to motherhood like a duck to water. While she fed her newborn, she informed me that she would be starting her exercise regime after bub's feed and she invited me to join her. She said, "I plan to walk the perimeter of the hospital!" I declined the invitation because quite honestly, I was struggling with the overwhelming role of 'new mum' and I also thought it would clash with afternoon tea. Just getting out of my pyjamas was going to be an effort!

She fed her bub, put on her walking shoes and then leant over her newborn and told her that she would be back in 20 minutes. She turned to me and said, "I can't wait to get out into the fresh air. I deserve this 'me' time and so does my body". Twenty minutes later, this new mum came bounding back into the room and said, "I feel amazing. I am reclaiming my body. How fantastic is that?" She then picked up her new baby and said, "I missed you! I am so grateful that I have you!"

At the same time, I was staring at my newborn baby boy, wondering if I had put his nappy on upside down! I was worried and scared of this tiny little person, and I was continuously filling my mind with 'what if-s'. My roommate, on the other hand, was constantly smiling, laughing and radiating love. She looked beautiful! I was looking drawn, tired, and overwhelmed, and I was causing undue stress to all those around me. I was creating enormous anxiety for myself, my baby and my husband! I was filling my mind with doubt and my body with comfort food, and when I was finally discharged from the hospital, I was a nervous wreck.

My weight gain and my negative thoughts took me to a place that was really foreign to me. I had always been a powerhouse, bursting with confidence. Before motherhood, I had hosted major fashion events in front of hundreds of people. I had modelled in fashion parades, and I never ever felt intimidated by anyone. I had always been self-assured because I constantly

CHAPTER TWELVE

told myself that I was completely comfortable with me. I would never shy away from a challenge, and the harder the challenge, the more determined I would be to come out shining, win or lose.

Somehow, my pregnancy, my weight gain and my new role as a mum overshadowed all that I once was. I had lost my sense of self-worth. After a few months of really soul-destroying negative thinking, I was certainly at my lowest. I felt really down, so I visited my family doctor. I had always been fond of him. He was from Singapore and was very practical. He never sugar-coated his words, and he was always honest with his diagnoses. He was simplistic and holistic with his treatments, unlike many others in his profession.

As I was feeling unwell, tired and depressed, a visit with him was definitely in order. I went to his surgery, sat down and told him my symptoms. He did his usual medical check-up and then sat back in his chair and said, "You are overweight! You are still eating for two and you are now one, plus you are being negative! I recommend you go home, reassess what you are putting into your body, take your baby for a walk and get some sunshine! Sunshine fixes everything".

I sat staring at him, and then I burst into tears. He was absolutely right. I felt somehow worse for just a moment because I had always been so totally together. How did I get here? How had I managed to get to such a low point? It had all happened in the blink of an eye. After a few minutes, I pulled myself together and headed home. Doc had given me the correct diagnosis, and I felt relieved. I had needed someone to point out what was black and what was white. It was definitely the right tonic for me.

From that day forward, I changed my diet. I would walk every morning with my gorgeous son in his pram. Sometimes

I would carry him in a sling for an extra-charged work out. I started reminding myself that I was healthy, happy and confident. I also acknowledged how lucky I was to have this gorgeous healthy boy. Little by little, I regained my inner strength. After I stopped stressing about motherhood and whether or not I was doing it correctly, I started to really love my new role as a mum. No longer did I look at every little tear and tantrum as a drama or a result of something I was doing incorrectly. I looked at every event as another funny little way of my son displaying his personality. Who cared if his nappy was not pinned perfectly? We all make mistakes. We are human. He was absolutely fine even with his nappy on upside down.

Everything became lighter and more enjoyable when I shifted my energy and focused on all that was great in my world. I went back to reminding myself daily of what a good job I was doing as a mum. I never criticised myself again, and from that moment onwards, I reclaimed my self-worth. The more confident I became, the healthier I felt. I had more energy to exercise, which in turn encouraged me towards a healthier body and lifestyle.

Interestingly enough, the more I moved forward, the more criticism I received from people. Have you ever noticed that when you embark on a diet, people instantly try to encourage you to eat the wrong foods? They persist in trying to tempt you to fail. "Oh go on, a little bit of that triple chocolate fudge cake with jam and cream won't hurt you." When you won't indulge, they then make comments to others about your obsession with your weight. Your ability to resist temptation somehow exposes their inability to change bad habits. By turning your positives into a negative, they feel empowered. It also makes them feel more self-confident to bring someone else down. These people, who attempt to strip others of their self-worth, tend to have extremely low self-esteem.

When I changed my attitude and focused on changing my life from down to up and my body from overweight to healthy, I encountered many people who would try to hinder me from continuing down the road to wellness. A negative comment from someone would instantly drag me back to that low place I was working so hard to leave behind.

I swiftly decided that I would never allow the negativity of others to affect my days again. I continue to practice this principle on a daily basis. When I was focusing on rebuilding my own self-esteem, I would always respond to a negative comment with a positive one. This instantly flat-lines the negative energy. When someone said to me once, "You have lost a lot of weight and are so thin," keeping in mind I had gone from heavily pregnant and eating for two to a perfectly healthy weight, I would simply respond with, "I have so much more energy now, and I have never felt better!"

I had a friend who would say, every time she saw me, "Oh gosh, you look so tired". I would meet her for coffee, and I would be feeling fabulous. She never failed to make that comment or something equally draining on one's soul, and as soon as she would say it, I would think, "Oh, yes. I am tired," and I would start to feel my energy levels fall.

She did it to all of her friends. Sometimes she would say you looked tired, and other days she would ask if you were sick. I heard her say to one of our friends on one occasion, "Oh, you are so quiet today. What is wrong with you? Are you ok? You look ill." Our friend was just fine but was trying hard to ensure she listened more to her friends when they were talking. She felt she needed to improve this skill.

Bringing other people down was my friend's way of making

herself feel more confident. She was rapidly losing friends, so I decided it was important that she understand why. Next time we met for coffee, she bounded in, and as soon as she sat down, I said, "Are you ok? You look exhausted today. What's wrong?" She stopped and sat for a minute, and then I saw her slump in her chair and heave a big sigh. She responded with, "Yes, I am a bit tired." Her whole demeanour changed from vibrant to fragile.

We met again the next day, and she walked into the cafe still looking miserable. When she sat down, I said to her, "You look amazing today!" She instantly sat up straight and started to smile and chat. I had boosted her self-esteem with four powerful positive words. I then proceeded to explain to her how her negative comments would affect us all. What I had done was simply put her in the same situation so that she could understand how depleting it was for many of us. It was the only way for her to comprehend the impact her words were having on us all.

My friend and I valued our friendship immensely. Enlightening her on how she was making me and the rest of our friends feel only served to make the relationship that much richer. From that day forward, she made a huge effort to highlight everyone's positive attributes. Shifting her focus to seeing the good in others came back to her tenfold. For every positive comment she gave out, she became more and more empowered and felt better about herself. She boosted her own self-esteem while boosting the self-esteem of those around her. It's important to choose your words wisely. They can make or break someone's day!

If you are suffering from low self-esteem, you have the power within you to change this instantly. Never criticise yourself or others. Reward your mind with powerful affirmations. I am confident, I am healthy, I am happy, I feel fantastic, I am good at my job, I am a great friend, I am a good mother, I am a good father, I am whole and complete, I am kind, I am understanding, I am worth it… The list is endless. Top up your tank with words that uplift your spirit and fuel you with positive energy.

Commit from this day forward to never self-criticise again. Self-criticism will bring you way down. Positive affirmations, on the other hand, will bring your energy levels way up and will improve your self-esteem. You will be overwhelmed by how much you can achieve, how good you will feel and how great you will make everyone else feel when you acknowledge your self-worth.

Shift your focus to seeing the good in you and also the good around you. Do everything in your power to acknowledge all of your good qualities. Positive thoughts are stepping stones that lead you to a more fulfilled life. What we think creates our reality. Love is the most powerful force of all. Learn to love yourself. You are worth it! You deserve it!

> *"You yourself, as much as anybody in the entire universe deserve your love & affection."*
> —**Buddha**

CHAPTER THIRTEEN
YOU Make the Miracles

When you are confident and have acknowledged your self-worth, it is mind-blowing what you are capable of achieving. There are simply no boundaries if you believe in yourself. I have a friend who is a full-time doctor. She volunteers at an animal shelter once a month. She is also a member of a cycling club, which cycles extremely long distances every Sunday morning. If that isn't enough, she is also a talented artist and has sold many of her paintings online. I am constantly in awe of her ability to multitask and live her life to the absolute fullest. How does she achieve so much? She never allows an obstacle to stop her from going forward. Nothing is impossible for this incredible lady. She also has a plethora of self-worth, which is surprising when you hear her story.

My friend and I grew up in the same suburb. We became great friends when we were around nine. Her parents were divorced, and her mother was an alcoholic. When she did spend time with her father, he verbally abused her and then returned her to her mum. Her parents continuously told her as a child that she was a waste of space, a mistake, ugly and stupid. If you ever wanted to witness an environment that was toxic and soul-destroying, you just had to pay a visit to her house. I will not refer to it as a 'home' for obvious reasons. She often came to my home after school. We would sit and play with my dolls and my dollhouse for hours. It was a great place for her to escape.

We lost contact over the years, and recently we managed to reconnect. After many inspiring discussions about life, goals and self-confidence, we focused on her past. She insisted that her upbringing had shaped her into who she was today. She had refused to be a victim of her family's weaknesses. She had said that as a child, she would keep telling herself that she was safe. When her family told her she was ugly, she would tell herself she was pretty. By the way, she was and still is extremely beautiful.

She would somehow cope with the sadness by taking herself to another place in her mind. She would visualise beautiful things—rivers and waterfalls, ballerinas and fairies—as far back as nine years old. She would picture herself inside my dollhouse every night before she fell asleep. She had to stay positive to survive her environment. She had to imagine that there would be a better place for her someday, and thankfully through sheer determination and focus, she has found it.

She acknowledges that the reason she lives such a full, rich life is due to choice. Her childhood encouraged her to choose a life of joy, fulfilment, kindness, success and understanding. Witnessing and experiencing the worst as a child only served to ensure that she would choose the best once she was able to move away from her family. She put herself through university and medical school to follow her dream of becoming a doctor.

She is a mum with two great kids. Her children are self-assured and also practice the "Life. Be in it" attitude that she has so adamantly instilled in them. She leads by example, and she constantly tells her children how much she loves them and how proud of them she is. I have heard them say exactly the same thing back to her without prompting, and it is always heartfelt.

She said to me that she is extremely grateful for her upbringing and constantly says thank you for the experience. Rather than hurting her, her childhood only served to strengthen and shape her into someone who will always be grateful for her blessed life. She is a mum, a doctor, an athlete, a friend, an artist and one hell of an inspiration to everyone!

Recently, while listening to the radio, I heard an interview with a woman who had just lost her thriving business because of a devastating fire. This business was family-owned and was started decades ago by her great-grandfather. The whole warehouse was burnt to the ground, along with the family home. The reporter had asked her what she planned to do now. You could hear the exhaustion in her voice from fighting to save her family's legacy, but she simply declared with great strength, "Although we have lost everything, thankfully no one was hurt. I ask that our loyal customers support us with patience while our family regroups and starts the business all over again. I promise we will come back better than ever." Many placed in similar circumstances would declare defeat and would only be able to focus on the devastation and loss. What a shining example that woman is of inner strength, power and the ability to see forward.

We all have the power to make miracles every day. The way to make miracles is to believe in your ability to succeed no matter what the obstacle. Find a way to go over it or around it because what's on the other side of the obstacle will bring you satisfaction and pure joy.

Never doubt your ability to succeed. Seeds of doubt sewn into your mind will manifest and create barriers that weaken your determination. These seeds are hard to uproot. Seeds bursting with positivity, on the other hand, will flourish and grow and manifest into your dreams. Don't wait for someone to come and change your life for you. You can do this for yourself. There are simply no limits if you believe in YOU!

"Miracles happen to those who believe in them."
— **Bernard Berenson**

CHAPTER FOURTEEN

The Power of Kindness

An act of kindness performed will bring great richness to your life as well as someone else's. The act when given freely with absolutely no expectations for anything in return will bring you immense peace and joy. When was the last time you did something that brought joy to someone else? If you have been too busy, it's worthwhile freeing up a little time and making it a priority. An act of kindness can truly change a person's day.

The universe is forever presenting opportunities to us in which we can choose to respond generously with kindness. Do you ignore these opportunities, or do you acknowledge them? Are you too overloaded to even see them? Imagine our world if everyone performed at least one act of kindness a day.

It shows great strength of character to continuously be kind. Those who practice kindness have better health, better quality of life and a calmness that comes with the ability to give without expectations. Those who give and always expect something back set themselves and others up for failure. A true act of kindness is performed from the heart. The only expectation from such a pure intention is to lift someone's spirits.

In today's stressful world, we are subject to more and more aggression. There is now more road rage, verbal abuse, bullying, violence and crime than ever before. Something has got to change. We can all make a difference in bringing more joy to this world. For every act of kindness you do, you give out an abundance of positive, warm, uplifting energy to the universe. There is no act of kindness too small. The simplest of gestures can affect many lives for the better.

Some weeks ago, I was standing in a checkout at the supermarket. There was an elderly woman in front of me. She was wearing a lovely floral dress and she had on a beautiful pink hat. Clearly, she had gone to great lengths to ensure she was looking her best. She was quite fragile, very frail, but still beautiful. She had done her weekly grocery shop, and while the checkout operator was scanning her items, she expressed her dismay at the cost of living and how hard it was to make ends meet.

While the checkout operator was packing her groceries up, the lovely old woman stood looking at a bucket of flowers at the end of the register. The bucket contained bouquets of carnations marked down to five dollars. She smiled and said, "Aren't they pretty? It has been a long time since I could afford flowers. My husband used to buy them for me, but he has gone now. They are just lovely, don't you think?" She smiled, thanked the checkout operator for her help and wished her a good day. Before she left the store, she stopped, bent down and smelt the flowers' scent one more time, and then she slowly pushed her trolley away.

I simply could not ignore the opportunity to give this lady the gift of kindness. I only had three items to check, so I picked out a pretty soft pink bouquet from the bucket and included it in my groceries. Within minutes my transaction was processed and I was heading out of the store.

The elderly lady was only a few metres away. Her pace was slow, and she used the trolley to support herself. I was overwhelmed at the number of men, women, teenagers and children who were pushing past her. They were almost knocking her over in their rush to get to wherever they needed to go. Regardless, this lovely old woman gently made her way through the chaos, still stopping to smile and acknowledge all those she passed.

I managed to catch up to her, and I introduced myself. I explained that I had been behind her in the grocery store and I saw her admiring the flowers and thought she would enjoy them in her home. Her face lit up. Her smile was radiant. She said, "Oh, I can't believe this! You have made my day. Thank you so much. This is wonderful."

I assisted her with her groceries, pushing her trolley to her car, and we chatted about her love of flowers and gardening. She was no longer able to get out and tend to her garden. The humidity associated with our tropical climate and her ageing body stopped her from what was once her passion. As she was leaving, she thanked me again. She continued to let me know that this simple act had lifted her spirits and warmed her heart. What she didn't realise was that she had reciprocated the same feeling back to me with her response. A kind word or an act performed with no expectations will contribute in a major way to changing our world's current energy.

Perhaps you know someone who just needs a chat and a cup of tea made for them. Maybe you could spare a minute and allow someone to go before you in the grocery queue if they only have a few items. Do you know someone who needs help cleaning out their shed? Whatever the act, small or large, if you invest a little of your time and energy, you will lift someone's spirits as well as your own. The healing powers of kindness are bountiful. I implore you to open up your heart and give generously from your ability to be kind. It will change your life and the lives of so many around you!

"Life's most urgent question is,
'What are you doing for others?'"
—**Martin Luther King**

CHAPTER FIFTEEN
Don't Play the Blame Game

If you are ready to do some cleaning up, clearing out and moving forward, it is important to acknowledge how and why things have fallen into disarray. If it is just a chaotic cupboard or a messy room that needs reorganising, acknowledge that perhaps it's just a lack of time and energy that has created the situation. Ensure that you delegate future time to keep on top of things once you have had your clean-up. If it is something much bigger than that, like our shed, make sure you confront and acknowledge the chaos. What does it all mean to you? When you are ready, take the necessary action to clean up and move forward. Ensure you learn and grow from the experience. A lesson learnt will enrich your life completely. It is very easy to blame other people for our messes, but playing the blame game never allows us to accept responsibility for our own actions. Take ownership of the journey. Sort out your mess, clean it up, acknowledge it and then move forward, only occasionally looking back to remind yourself of how far you have come.

I once counselled a woman who had come to me to lose weight and reclaim her life. She had been through a nasty break-up and was heartbroken. Her now ex-husband had an affair with a much younger woman during their marriage. Her self-esteem was battered, and each night after the break up, she cried and ate herself to sleep. When her tears dried up and her local supermarket had sold out of rum raisin

Haagen-Dazs ice-cream, she looked in the mirror and did not recognise the person staring back at her. She had gained 15 kilos and she was emotionally and physically exhausted. When we began our consultation, she had initially started the session with her ex-partner's infidelity.

She used our time to really verbalise her anger towards him, completely ensuring that he was responsible for every single kilo gained. After she got it all out of her system, I said to her, "You have completely focused on the hurt your ex-husband has caused you for a long time now. By doing this, you have successfully taken yourself to this very low point. This destructive energy that you have consumed yourself with since the breakup—has it been worth three more dress sizes?" She sat contemplating my question and responded firmly with, "Absolutely not."

We talked about her journey to this dark place as well as the hurt she was still feeling. While she consumed herself with anger every day and blamed her ex-husband for the break-up, she managed to completely drown herself in misery. I gently shifted her focus back to the beginning of their relationship. I asked her to list all the positive things that she had experienced during their marriage. During this exercise, her demeanour changed from exhausted to peaceful.

She had travelled all over the world with this man. Through him, she had met amazing people whom she now considers lifelong friends. He had supported and encouraged her to get a university degree. His encouragement had motivated her to achieve her goals and embark on a very fulfilling career. They had shared some incredibly happy times together. When she focused on the positives and acknowledged her gratitude for the experiences, she instantly felt a sense of calm. She definitely did not want to reunite with him, so it was well and truly time to move on.

CHAPTER FIFTEEN

The final few years of their marriage together had become difficult for both of them. They seemed to just naturally grow apart. Her ex-husband initially struggled to tell her of his affair because of the longevity of their relationship. In his eyes, he had just made a big mistake and it seemed easier to keep it quiet. He had thought that perhaps his guilt would eventually subside, but it just consumed him, and he finally opened up to her and revealed his indiscretion. We certainly did not applaud him for his infidelity, but no one can change the past, so it was really important for her to let go of the anger as it was destroying her soul. Once she reviewed the whole experience with clearness, clarity and an open heart, she was able to see forward. She felt released from the pain and was now ready for a new beginning.

Deciding to lose weight, get fit and work on healing herself gave her new purpose. A few days later, she emailed me to let me know that she had made the decision to call her ex-husband after our session. She had insisted that she had really felt an urgency to make peace with him. She offered him friendship and wished him happiness for his future. She acknowledged all that they had once shared and thanked him for the experience. He reciprocated, and to this day, they have a renewed friendship. By the way, she has lost 20 kilos, has opened her own business and has never been happier. She is strong, independent and happily single!

If an experience in life doesn't quite turn out the way you envisage, you have a choice when it comes to how you respond to the situation. On the one hand, you can criticise and blame others and keep rehashing over the events. In return, you will receive destructive negative energy for your efforts, bringing yourself and all those around you down. On the other hand, you can choose to respond to a negative situation by showing strength of character, integrity, dignity, intelligence and humility, and this will lead to growth and expansion for you as a person. Acknowledging what you have learnt from the experience and how you have benefited from the process will allow you to clear out the mess from the situation and use the good from it for future growth.

How we take part in life's journey and how we arrive at the destination depends on how we view each crossroad. It's your life and your choice—no one else's. Choose how you respond to every situation wisely as this choice will always affect the final outcome. When you live your life with an open heart, you allow endless possibilities to present themselves. Ensure you are not consumed with negativity so that you can hear, see and feel these opportunities when they arrive.

Make changes, not excuses! Now is the time to acknowledge what it is that might be stopping you from living your life to its full potential. Clearing out all the blockages, whether they are material items or emotional baggage from our lives, allows us to heal on so many different levels.

If you want to change your life's direction, nothing is better than a good clean-up! It is therapeutic, uplifting, enlightening and life changing! Make it your focus to ensure that there is a clear pathway for life's joyous energy to come flooding into your world.

Dream big, be patient, laugh loudly, cherish your loved ones, trust yourself, be kind, live simply, smile and if your shed needs a clean-up, don't waste another minute—DO IT NOW!

"We are shaped by our thoughts; we become what we think. When the mind is pure, joy follows like a shadow that never leaves."
—**Buddha**

PART TWO

Your 10 Steps Forward

What do you need to clean out? Is it your home, your mind, your body or your shed? Perhaps there are many areas in your life that require attention. Most of us have the ability to clutter up our lives with objects and emotions. Whether we like it or not, we all hold onto things that stop us from moving forward. These things take up a lot of space, creating obstacles and distractions. They also consume a lot of our very precious energy. Physically, we clutter up our homes, our offices and our bodies. Emotionally, we clutter up our minds with thoughts, feelings and reactions. Spiritually, we clutter up our hearts and souls with emotional debris. How can we live a peaceful existence if our home is a mess? How can we be emotionally calm if we are consumed with negative thoughts? How can we find our life's purpose if we are unable to feel or trust our own intuition?

It is liberating, empowering and uplifting to sort through all of our mess and clean it up! It frees us from the heaviness that accompanies clutter and allows us to see clearly. Mess, no matter what form it takes, is all encompassing. It is multi-layered and heavy.

It is vital to acknowledge the mess in your life and take those all-important steps to free yourself from its limitations. It is important to stop thinking of clearing out the mess as a tremendous, overwhelming task. Instead, start thinking of it as one of the most vital self-improvement tactics you can possibly do.

The journey forward starts with a single step.

Step One: *Clean Up Your House*

Harmony at home

Your first step forward should begin with your living space. Creating a more peaceful, organised environment will restore balance and allow the positive energy to gently flow back into your world.

Stop and breathe

Mentally prepare yourself to start this cleansing journey by breathing deeply and acknowledging that you are ready and willing to make these changes. Open up your home's windows and doors, allowing fresh air and new energy to flow in. Walk through your home with your eyes wide open. Have a good long look inside every room. Are your rooms cluttered and messy? Are you hoarding unnecessary items? Be brutally honest with your living space. If all you can see is clutter and mess, it's time to commit to a big clean up.

One space at a time

If you are slightly overwhelmed by the enormity of the job ahead, there is a simple plan of attack that will ensure success: Start with one room at a time. Throw out useless items and discard unnecessary bits and pieces that have just sat dormant for years. Be honest—not emotional—when deciding what you will keep and what you will discard. If you have items that you simply must hang on to, put them into storage boxes and label them so they are easily accessible. Once you have completely decluttered one space, move on to the next.

Pace yourself

Cleaning up your home doesn't all have to be done in one day; it can be done over a period of time. Even if you focus on cleaning just one area in a single room per day, you will soon start to feel the energy shift, and calm and organisation will gently flow back into your life. Commit to finishing one room completely before you move on to the next. Don't flip from room to room. It has taken years to collect all the contents in your home—the good and the bad. Pace yourself with the clean-up so you don't burn out and only half complete the task.

Phone a friend

If you are struggling to do the clean-up alone, recruit family and friends to help you complete the job. Be sure that you do not recruit assistants who will encourage you to keep what you need to discard. If you have items that are in reasonable condition but you no longer use, consider having a garage sale or perhaps donating them to Goodwill. Reward your friends and family with a celebration at the end of the clean-up. Have a barbeque or party with the profits from your garage sale and celebrate your new beginning!

Warm up your space

When you have reorganised your home, bring in some candles, scented oils and flowers to breathe life, warmth and love into your newly cleansed environment. It is magical when you replace clutter with elements that will allow you to experience the scent of a new beginning, such as the glow of a soft candle and the colour and beauty of a flowering plant. Give your space wings!

Stop, look and listen

Little by little, as you clear all the clutter, you will allow the light to start filtering through. You simply cannot ignore the calmness that accompanies organisation. The benefits of it are enormous. Clear out and clean up to release the blockages and allow a positive inflow of uplifting energy into your home.

Step Two: *Clear Out Your mind*

Identify the noise

Unnecessary noise often blocks us from hearing life's lovely rhythm. Mind noise can become overwhelming, often making it difficult to focus and see clearly. The distraction from this continuous chatter of the mind can often lead to our experiencing great anxiety. The mind often repeats the same thoughts over and over again. If they are positive thoughts, that is fine, but more often than not, the thoughts are negative ones that cause us to continuously rehash over the difficulties we may be experiencing.

Stop and identify your thoughts. What are you filling your mind with?

Work noise

At some stage of our working lives, most of us have experienced an employer who considers it their right to overwork their employees. As an employee, little regard is often given to your privacy or your personal life. Often, you tolerate these conditions because of your financial commitments and the difficulty of finding alternative employment. What's the old saying? "Better the devil you know!" If you find yourself in this situation, the mind noise from the overload is continuous.

When we are tolerating a situation that is stepping over the boundaries of what is acceptable, duties are often done reluctantly. In the process, we are continuously verbalising our dissatisfaction in our minds. We can't verbalise it out loud because the unemployment queues nowadays are particularly lengthy.

Emotional overload

Ever had a 'friend' who constantly uses you as a sounding board? They are only interested in talking about their own lives. They are not remotely interested in talking about you. After they have unleashed their lot in life onto you, they feel a sense of relief, but you are exhausted. After the experience, you are left with your mind in overdrive, trying to process their problems. Someone once said to me that if you have a friend who has a more negative impact than a positive impact on your life, they are not truly a friend. Worth considering, I think!

Family fiasco

Some family members consider it their birthright to ensure that their entire family supports them through every single one of life's hurdles. Now, don't get me wrong here—we all have challenges, and there is nothing more comforting than family support, but what about that family member who creates their own drama day in and day out and then expects you to clean up their mess? I think most of us at some point can look at our family tree and see someone who displays this quality.

Can you relate?

Just trying to fit everyday demands into your schedule can cause the mind to go into overdrive. You can't hear yourself think. Wherever the noise is coming from, ensure you identify it. It's important to stop the harassing negative thoughts before you are completely overloaded. When that mental noise subsides, your focus will become deeper and clearer.

Turn that switch OFF

If the noise is all consuming, it's time to turn it down. How do we eliminate this noise and clear our minds? The first step is to simply STOP. Be conscious of what you are focusing your thoughts on. Practice concentration. Focus completely on a thought that is uplifting. If your mind starts to wander, quickly refocus on the initial positive thought. Work daily on strengthening your ability to concentrate. Meditation will close the mind to distracting and negative thoughts. You don't need to be a yogi to meditate! A few minutes of meditation each day will calm down the mental noise and bring you closer to inner-peace. Start with 10 slow deep breaths. This will automatically bring your mind and body back into balance. Just breathing and focusing on your breath will quickly induce a meditative state. You will feel centred, and it will be easier to focus. Just like with a radio, you can turn this noise up or turn it down.

Concentrate on filling your mind with all that is positive in your world and tune into those thoughts. Go for a quick walk in the fresh air to settle your mind down. It's hard to feel anxious when you surround yourself with nature, and separating from a negative environment will recharge the soul and clear your mind. The more conscious you become about your mind's thoughts, the better your life will become. Stop the negative noise and your senses will function better.

Put up a stop sign

Set boundaries for friends, family and work commitments. It's fine to close down our computers and turn off our phones on the weekend and after hours. Email, social media and texting are all continuous lifelines to people. It seems now that we are available 24/7 to everyone.

Many are addicted to social media. Some are so focused on it that they are consumed more with other people's lives than their own. If this sounds like you, commit to turning off your phones and Internet when you are at home. Allow your mind to rest and re-focus on peace and quiet. If it is too difficult to completely shut down your phones and emails, allocate certain times for checking them. Make some rules about how long you will spend reviewing messages, and be vigilant about adhering to them. For example, just dedicate one hour a day on the weekend to checking your email and messages and that is it!

The shutdown icon is on the left-hand side of your computer

What would happen if you didn't check your Facebook account for a few days? The answer is 'absolutely nothing!' When you go back to checking your account eventually, you will just scroll through endless comments about the weather, the parties and the dramas that your friends so publically expose!

Turn off your mobile

What would happen if you turned off your phone? People would most likely leave a message if they needed to contact you urgently, and then you could choose and control whom you wish to respond to!

It's your choice

It sounds easy doesn't it? Well, it is. If you are bombarded with mindless noise, turn it off. Your mind is like a garden bed. For every negative thought you plant, it manifests. A negative thought is similar to a weed. It spreads and quickly takes over.

Make it a rule to weed out your mind every few hours. Plant positive seeds through affirmations, and your mind will flourish! Don't underestimate the power of your thoughts. Just as your thoughts can escalate stress, they can also relieve stress.

Step Three: *Clean Out Your Body*

When did it all become so complicated?

Food used to be simple. At one time, you ate what you grew yourself on your own land or what you purchased from farmers. Processed and fast food wasn't an option. Today, food is far more complicated in more ways than we can imagine, and in some ways we are both better and worse off for it! It's very easy to mistreat our bodies with a poor diet. Our bodies are quite resilient, but at some stage, if we disrespect them too much, they will let us know!

You are what you eat

If you are feeling bloated and overweight, it is vital to take stock of what it is that you are consuming. Bad diets laden with sugar, salt and saturated fats have led us to an obesity crisis. If you are feeling weighed down, it is time for a health check and food overhaul! It is worth it to feel your energy levels soar and your general well-being improve.

The media has confused us!

Low fat, low GI, high protein, meal replacements, soup diets, and weight loss pills—the choices are endless. There are so many diets available today that it can get overwhelming. If you are confused about losing weight and boosting your energy levels, consider scrapping diets and opt for healthy eating instead.

Write it down

Writing down everything you eat for a week is a great way to address any problem areas. You will be amazed at just what and how much you are consuming when you start recording it. Keeping a food journal is a fantastic, motivating first step towards eating healthier foods. Once you begin making positive nutritional choices, you will get great satisfaction when you review your healthy food diary. You will understand completely why you are feeling better!

Down-size

It's not only what we are eating but also how much we are eating. Our plate sizes have grown considerably since the 1960s. An average dinner plate in the 60s was 8.5 inches. Our average plate size now is around 12 inches and the bigger your portion sizes, the bigger your calorie intake. Before you know it, you've taken in 20–30 per cent more calories than you actually should at a meal. This really adds up over time and starts to show up on your waistline.

Keep it simple

Keeping it simple is a great principle and should be applied to our diets. Have three meals a day and be sure to keep them well-balanced. Each meal should consist of a small serving of protein, and the rest of the meal should largely include vegetables and some grains.

Choose fish as your protein and restrict red meat to once a week. Include two pieces of fruit a day. Drink copious amounts of filtered water and green tea. Limit alcohol consumption to two standard drinks a day and ensure you have at least two drink-free nights a week. If you can eliminate alcohol all together, well, cheers to you! Move briskly for 30 minutes a day.

When grocery shopping, focus on purchasing from the perimeter of the supermarket. You will find fresh seafood, lean meat, poultry, dairy, fruit and vegetables all on the outside rim of the store. In the central aisles, you will find all of the foods with human interference. Snack foods, biscuits, soft drinks and other items loaded with salt, sugar, fats, Trans fats, preservatives, additives and many other nasties that our bodies struggle to break down.

Realistically, these items are not food. When thinking of food, train your mind to see food as organic, fresh, wholesome, colourful and clean, and associate this food with energy, healthy weight management and anti-ageing. Discover pleasure in eating real food!

Clean out your pantry and your fridge

Don't wait until you have consumed all of the bad food in your pantry before you change your eating habits. As soon as you have made the commitment to change, immediately discard any unhealthy foods that will cause temptation and sabotage your healthy eating regime. Fill your fridge with nutritious foods, fruits and vegetables.

Visit your general practitioner

It's important to be responsible for your health and have regular health checks. Your GP can check conditions like diabetes, blood pressure and cholesterol and can help you set realistic goals when it comes to overhauling your diet.

Eat to live

It's common knowledge that centenarians in Okinawa follow a diet that consists of fish, vegetables, legumes, fruits, filtered water and green tea. They consume plenty of fibre and antioxidants. Many Westerners, on the other hand, consume unhealthy calorie-packed diets and rarely exercise. They are writing their own prescriptions for heart disease and early mortality.

Respect your body

Acknowledge that your body must go the distance and you must nurture, support and maintain it so it functions at its best. It is the only body you have to take you through this life. Be sure to treat it with the respect it deserves and appreciate all it does for you!

Step Four: *Spring Clean Your Soul*

Shining brightly

We are all conscious of our minds, bodies and souls. When you think of the mind and the body, it's crystal clear as to what they both are, but when you think of your soul, it's a little harder to define or locate. When thinking of your soul, imagine it is your central light source, located near your heart! Your soul generates energy, warmth, compassion, forgiveness, and kindness. It's your inner-light. It's your core essence. It's what makes you uniquely you. The soul is the essence of humanity's being; it is who we are!

Is your inner light shining brightly?

When your soul is full of warmth, it shines brightly, radiating love to all those you encounter. If your soul is depleted due to life's overwhelming challenges, it is often the case that it is difficult to see the good in any situation. Have you ever met someone who 'lights up a room'? They radiate a light that flows out and energises everyone around them. Their soul shines brightly. Having a positive, compassionate and forgiving outlook on life continuously refuels the soul.

How can you tell if your soul is depleted?

If you are seeing the worst in every situation, if you are constantly verbalising how bad life is and if you are feeling hopeless and despairing, then it is definitely time to find new ways to recharge your soul.

Shine brightly from within

Take some time out to experience peace and calm. Make a commitment to finding your passion. Find the purpose in your life. If you have a dream, plan the course of its journey. Have faith that you can create a more fulfilling life. Be bold, be brave, and be thankful that you can change your life's course in a heartbeat. Finding your passion will instantly fire up your soul!

Focus and shift your vision

Take every opportunity to show kindness and compassion. Look for life's endless possibilities at every turn. Find the good in every situation. Don't see difficult challenges as bad luck; instead, ask yourself what it is that you can learn from the experience. When you encounter difficult people, do not resent them. Behind every difficult person is another lesson to be learnt. It's through our toughest times that we learn what we are made of. Be grateful for all those who bring you joy and love. Family, children, friends, pets — they continuously add joyous fuel to our souls. Give selflessly and expect nothing in return. The act of giving lights up so many lives and also gives a hearty dose of energy to your own soul!

Your soul is your essence

So how do you spring clean your soul and ensure your light is burning continuously?

It's simple!
Here is your recipe:
Two heaped cups of patience
One heart full of love
Ten hands full of generosity
Five cups of genuine compassion
One cup of LOUD heartfelt laughter
One head full of understanding
Sprinkle generously with kindness and peace
Add plenty of faith, and mix well
Spread over a period of a lifetime and serve to everyone you ever encounter!
Author for this recipe ~ Unknown

Step Five: *Focus on What You Have*

Acknowledgement

Most of us are continuously focusing on all that we want and not on what we already have. It is vital to set positive goals and have dreams for the future, but before you set this vision, ask yourself, "When was the last time I stopped and said thank you for all that is currently in my life?" Now is the perfect time to count your blessings.

Do you have children?

It can be exhausting being a parent. We have to balance work, home, parenting, tantrums, and education, and we have to do it all without breaking a sweat! Occasionally, we are confronted by well-meaning friends and relatives advising us that we are doing it incorrectly. Parenting can be quite overwhelming. There is no manual supplied when our angels arrive. They laugh, play, throw tantrums, get dirty, eat, don't eat and do it all when it just feels right for them. They can't always adjust their emotional state to fit into our busy schedules.

As tiring as it can be sometimes, every day is a day lost if you don't see your children for who they are. They are just little tiny people trying to keep up with the grownups! Be grateful for every minute you have with your children. They are gifts from God and the most precious part of every single day. You only have to look into your child's eyes every morning to see how much love radiates from their little heart. When you are having an exhausting day with your little ones, spare a thought for the many that cannot have children or have lost their children. You can never give your child too much love or too many hugs!

I want to be thinner!

I have been privileged to work with many people, assisting them in achieving a healthy body with a balanced diet. Often, women will come to me and acknowledge that it is time to get healthy and lose weight, and I applaud them. More often than not, a woman in her 50s will come to me, and I will ask her, "What do you think you should weigh?" She will always reply with a goal weight that is unachievable. I always remind her of the journey her body has been on in the last 30 or so years. I encourage her to focus on letting her body go to where it is supposed to go naturally with healthy eating. That may be a size 12 instead of a size 8, but it is still healthy and beautiful. If you have been blessed with a fuller figure, accept your shape and work on making it feel more beautiful with a healthy lifestyle. Be proud of your body and appreciate its beauty. Treat it with respect and walk proudly in it. Love your shape!

I hate my job

If you are really unhappy with your current employment, start taking steps to change it. Open up your world to new opportunities by studying after work. Consider making plans to explore other job opportunities. As difficult as it may seem, be grateful for the income it is giving you. It may not be exactly what you want, but at least you have a job and a pay cheque. If the boss is hard work, remember that they shoulder the majority of the responsibility and often reflect this with a short fuse! It's no excuse, though. A great leader rarely loses their cool and leads and inspires their team by example.

Acknowledge all of the positive things you have learnt at your current position. Consider all of the productive contributions you make to your place of employment in a single day. Before you start work in the morning, be sure to remind yourself that you will have a good day despite the pressures. Commit to working with grace, dignity and efficiency. Smile and spread as much positivity as you can amongst your colleagues. Tell yourself that this is just a stepping stone to a better, brighter opportunity.

Be grateful for your current employment. There are so many people around the world struggling to find a job. Many would gladly exchange 'no money' for 'some money' and the opportunity to have a place to go every day to make a difference. Be innovative and think big. If you can't find a job, maybe you can create one! Don't underestimate the power of sheer determination. Be grateful.

Focus on what is in front of you RIGHT NOW!

Think of all the people who are currently in your life and whom you appreciate and love. Say their names out loud and give thanks for the privilege of not being alone.

Do you have a roof over your head and a warm bed? Give thanks that you are not homeless.

Are you healthy? Give thanks for your health. There are so many people in the world currently struggling with health issues and disabilities who still manage to view their challenges as just that— a challenge. Do you have enough food to feed yourself and your family? According to the Food and Agriculture Organization of the United Nations there are nearly a billion people starving in the world today. Worse still, 19 million of those are children under five years of age.

If you are surrounded by loved ones and are warm, healthy and not hungry, acknowledge your blessings and give thanks. Gratitude and humility are two qualities that will ensure you travel through this life blessed!

Step Six: *Write it Down*

See your future

Making a plan for your future is vital in order to bring your dreams to reality. Before you do this, however, you need to acknowledge your achievements to date and be proud of them. Be grateful for all that you have experienced and all that you have learnt. It is important to recognise all that you have accomplished and the journey you have been on before you go on the next one. I have a huge whiteboard in my office. At the beginning of each year, I write in list form what I wish to achieve over the next 12 months. Looking at this board daily helps with my direction. I can see where I am heading!

What's on my board?

My board has a wide and yet varied set of goals for the year. Travel, more exercise, renovating the bathroom — these are just some of the things on my board. I have also included images of how I would like to see my future unfold and the direction I want to see my future move in both personally and professionally. Health, spirituality, relationships—nothing is off limits on my list.

Acknowledge your goals

Each morning, I take a moment to review my board and the list of goals I have set. It keeps me focused and on track. Whenever I succeed in achieving one of my goals, I mark it off with a big tick! I have everything in order of priority. This gives me direction and a plan to follow. Once I achieve one of my goals, I acknowledge my success and give thanks for the journey that it has taken me on.

How long is your list?

No list is too long. I try to set myself a 12-month period for achieving my goals, but my list is always extensive. When I review my list at the end of the 12 months, there are normally still goals that have not been achieved. I simply keep those written on the board and make them a priority for the following 12 months.

Half a list achieved is still success

I have never ever looked at my list and felt disappointed that only half of the goals were achieved in the set time. Each goal completed is a massive step forward and should be celebrated. Every one of them, when completed, has bought more learning into my life.

Set your goals for the future today

I encourage you to write a list of your goals. Ensure you place your list in a highly visible spot so you are continuously reminded of where you are heading. With the right mental attitude, nothing will stop you from achieving your dreams.

Step Seven: *Stay Focused*

You have to work at it!

It can be challenging to stay motivated and focused all of the time. Life's constant distractions will keep coming. Just don't allow them to stop you from achieving a brighter, happier future.

Overload

Acknowledge that you are human and it's normal to lose focus. Take time out when you need it. If you are meditating but can't concentrate, just stop and try again tomorrow. If you are just too worn out to climb that hill on your exercise track, walk on the flat path!

Listen to your body. Listen to your mind. Just don't abandon your commitments completely because of a few challenges.

Pace yourself. Often when you feel overloaded, just taking a break for an hour or two will give you the energy to refocus.

The secret to staying focused

In regards to your life path, your goals and your daily life, how do you stay focused? Just keep going! When you fall, get back up. Re-evaluate daily and break your goals and plans up into more manageable pieces. Prioritise constantly to keep it all balanced. Little by little, you will achieve what you are aiming for. If you have had a bad day, let it go and prepare for tomorrow. Keep your pathways clear. Remove the mess so you can keep moving forward.

A new day

Just as the world continues to turn, a new day brings endless opportunities. A new day generates renewed energy and hope. You choose how you will respond to the day's events, so the first few minutes and hours of your day are the most important ones. Your mind is awake and receptive to anything that comes along, so feed yourself positive thoughts to effectively start your new day with endless possibilities.

Step Eight: *Repel Negative Energy*

Bring everyone up or take everyone down

Have you ever met someone who makes you feel down? They are continuously moody, negative and self-absorbed. When you are in their presence, they make you feel miserable and exhausted.

CHAPTER FIFTEEN

Going down

Often considered emotional vampires, these negative people drain you, not of blood but of every last drop of emotional energy. It's almost surreal how easily these individuals can get you to trust them and then, just as quickly, they suck the life right out of you.

No one has the right to bring you down in any way, shape or form!

Try to imagine that a negative person is surrounded by a dark cloud. This dark cloud gets thicker and heavier as their destructive behaviour gets more intense. The cloud spreads and overshadows all those in its presence. The deep, dark fog pulls you in. The deeper you get drawn into it, the worse you feel. To avoid getting caught in this emotional deluge, you need to rise above the darkness!

Going up

It's actually easier than you think to go up and stay up! Staying up makes you and everyone around you feel better. Start your day with a ritual. As you rise, acknowledge all of the positives in your life and give thanks. Take some time to either meditate or exercise before you begin your day. If possible, do both! Exercising in the morning will energise your body and instantly lift you up! Meditation will calm your mind, enabling you to think and see clearly.

If time does not permit, exercise in the morning and meditate in the evening. Commit to having a good day upon rising no matter what you encounter. Reinforce your mind with positive affirmations. *I am safe, I am protected, I am happy, I am confident, I am loved, I am successful, I will accept all that comes my way today with an open heart, I will respond to all that I encounter with understanding, respect and kindness.* Each positive affirmation you make reinforces your strength and protects you from the negative energy that we often encounter in our lives.

Staying up

Prepare yourself for a day of positive flow no matter what the challenge. Do not allow anyone to bring you down. You may feel yourself slowly being drawn into someone else's dark cloud over the course of the day. As soon as you feel that happening, refocus! Begin saying your positive affirmations in your mind. Stay completely detached from the person who is creating the problem. Imagine that you are surrounded by a white light that encases you and repels negative energy. Stay completely focused on your own energy at all times and safeguard yourself from the destructive force. Quietly and calmly, lift your spirits up by affirming and finding a positive in every situation! UP is a great place to be!

Are you causing inclement weather?

Perhaps you are the one causing the storms. Perhaps you are the eye of the cyclone. Do you bring rain, dark clouds, storms and mass destruction to all those in your world? Wouldn't you rather bring warmth, sunshine, calmness and joy to the people around you? If you are currently spreading darkness, shake it off. You can instantly start to dispel the dark clouds by focusing on taking yourself up! You will feel a whole lot safer and happier when you experience the warmth of a sunny disposition!

Step Nine: *Soften Your Focus*

What is soft focus?

If you choose to soften the way you look at life, you will find that life's journey is much gentler. Soft focus means that you have the ability to view every situation with a compassionate heart. Focusing softly on every situation before reacting allows you time to evaluate the event. Shifting your vision to be more emotionally intelligent, empathetic and caring will open up a new level of mindfulness.

Adjusting your view to soft focus

Instead of focusing on the worst of a situation, find the positives in the event and focus on those points intensely. Practice optimism. There are enormous mental health benefits to being optimistic. Those who soften their focus and are optimistic and compassionate suffer less stress, are more confident about the future, cope better with challenges and experience more joy and personal contentment. It takes practice and patience, but if you commit to finding a positive outcome to every situation, you can enjoy the benefits of soft focus.

How full is your glass?

"Is the glass half empty, or half full?" This is a common saying meaning we all should take a moment to evaluate how we see and react to things. I am constantly humbled by people in challenging situations who continuously look at life with compassion, optimism and a gentle approach. They never see a difficult circumstance as a problem. They will always turn every situation into a victory.

The focus may be soft, but the view is crystal clear

Your mind will create and manifest according to the images you habitually think about. Your thoughts and responses are the primary creative forces in your life. Use them consciously, and your future will become crystal clear.

Step Ten: *Start Your Affirmations and Change Your Life*

Plant powerful words in your mind and watch them grow

Positive affirmations will enhance your world. Continuously filling your mind with what is right and not what is wrong will allow you to experience a higher vibration. Vibration is energy. The secret to living a life that is intellectually, physically, emotionally and spiritually vibrant is to strive for very high vibrations. Developing a positive mindset is one of the most powerful life strategies known to man.

Continuously repeating affirmations with conviction and passion will chip away at even the most negative of souls. Words are powerful. Be sure to choose your words wisely as they create your thoughts and life experiences.

CHAPTER FIFTEEN

Positive affirmations will reprogram your mind, so what are you waiting for?

I am safe.
I am supported.
I deserve love.
I am loving.
I am loved.
I am happy.
I am peaceful.
I am protected.
I believe in myself.
I am strong.
I am calm.
I am unique.
Life is joyous.
I am open to change.
I accept change.
My body is energetic.
My body is healthy.
I approve of myself.
I deserve prosperity
I am deserving.
I am grateful.
I am successful.
I trust.
I will succeed.
I will have an amazing day.
I can.
I will.
I am free.
I am surrounded by love.
I am in control of my life.
Thank you for my life.

...the list is endless!

Create your own affirmations

Spend some time focusing on what areas of your life need improving. Think about how you want to feel. It is worth really spending time on this process. Once you have acknowledged all of the positive emotions and experiences you want to bring into your life, write them down. For every point you have written down on your list, write a positive statement. The statement should be written in the present tense, focusing on improving and enhancing confidence, well-being and your life as a whole.

Word power

Affirmations reprogram your thought patterns, bring positive change into your life and allow growth and healing. Say and think your affirmations with passion and conviction. These words are so powerful that they will instantly change your life for the better!

Thank You

Two very powerful words

Saying 'thank you' will instantly release the ties that bind our souls tightly and block us from acknowledging the blessings in our lives. Experiencing gratitude and giving thanks for all that we have and all that we receive will open the floodgates to the universal stream of goodness.

I want to thank you for taking the time to read *The Shed*. I am grateful that you have picked up my book and allowed me

CHAPTER FIFTEEN

the privilege of sharing some of my life lessons and experiences with you. We have so much to deal with and so much to fit into our everyday lives that it is easy to lose track of it all. One day, you realise that you are so consumed with the emotional and physical mess that it is difficult to know how to fix it all.

Organising our lives, clearing up the mess, acknowledging past failures, accepting challenges, changing our attitude, shifting our vision, giving thanks, trusting our own intuition, being brave—these are all positive life-changing actions that we should strive to include in our everyday living. Whether you have a physical mess that needs clearing or an emotional mess that needs addressing, know that you have the power deep within you to change any situation.

This unbelievable power that we all possess is accessible right now. Universal challenges may have diminished your strength and life's dust may have settled on your soul, but you have the ability to clean this up.

Take a step forward every day and live life to the fullest. You have everything you need right now to create an incredible life, but you must take action. It isn't hard; it isn't complicated! It's actually very simple! Don't let a little mess stop you from seeing, feeling and accepting life's goodness.

I wish for all those who read this book a lifetime of endless
possibilities, the freedom to choose, an open heart,
soft focus and...a tidy shed!

In the words of Joseph Swift,
"May you live all the days of your life."
Thank You